HITLER'S
LAST SOLDIER
IN AMERICA

Also by Arnold Krammer:

Nazi Prisoners of War in America
The Forgotten Friendship: Israel and the Soviet Bloc, 1947-1953

HITLER'S LAST SOLDIER
IN AMERICA

GEORG GAERTNER
with Arnold Krammer

sd

STEIN AND DAY/*Publishers*/New York

Author's note:
A small number of names and places have been changed to protect the privacy of
individuals.

First published in 1985
Copyright © 1985 by Georg Gaertner
All rights reserved. Stein and Day, Incorporated
Designed by Louis A. Ditizio
Printed in the United States of America
STEIN AND DAY/*Publishers*
Scarborough House
Briarcliff Manor, N.Y. 10510

Library of Congress Cataloging in Publication Data

Gaertner, Georg, 1920–
  Hitler's last soldier in America.

  Includes index.
    1. Gaertner, Georg, 1920–   2. World War,
1939–1945—Prisoners and prisons, American.   3. Prisoners
of war—Germany—Biography.   4. Prisoners of war—
United States—Biography.   5. Escapes—United States.
I. Krammer, Arnold, 1941–   II. Title.
D805.U5G34   1985   940.54′72′73   84-40622
ISBN 0-8128-3007-5

CONTENTS

ILLUSTRATIONS

School graduation photo
In Alpine hat and leather coat, c. 1940
The Gaertner family, 1940
Playing tennis in Schweidnitz, 1935
Ski talk, 1933
The ski lodge, 1933–1939
Skiing, mid-1930s
With Horst Trispel
At a German Labor Service Camp, 1939–40
As a German Labor Service volunteer
Wehrmacht basic training
On promotion to lance corporal
On maneuvers
As a sergeant in Rommel's Afrika Korps
Officer candidate Georg Gaertner in Wehrmacht dress uniform
A troop train en route to Greece
Athens Gypsy predicting "a long trip"
Bathing in the Adriatic Sea
Boarding a transport plane to North Africa, 1942
Dugout near Tripoli, 1943
FBI wanted poster
FBI photos
As a ski teacher
Teaching tennis in California

With the German "countess"
With friends
The snowbound *City of San Francisco* streamliner
On the rescue mission
Parents in Germany, 1956
Newspaper ad soliciting my whereabouts
With columnist Herb Caen
With tennis star Vic Seixas
With screen star Robert Stack
With Bjorn Borg and doubles partner
With Lloyd Bridges at Aspen
The pro shop
At Alamo Pro-Am Tournament
Painting in Hawaii
In a bookstore
With wife Jean, 1985
With new car, 1985
In New Mexico, 1985
With Professor Arnold Krammer

ACKNOWLEDGMENTS

I can imagine few life-styles more difficult to record than that of a fugitive. Names and addresses change with regularity. Secrecy is all-important. Someone living in fear of arrest seldom saves receipts, records, or diaries. Close friendships are a liability and therefore shed little light on feelings and motives. The chronicler then turns to the official agencies engaged in the hunt, the FBI and the U.S. Army, to find only limited information. After all, they were unable to catch the fugitive. From an historian's viewpoint such a sparsity of documentation makes the writing of a book particularly difficult.

Fortunately, I had the help of experts. First, my thanks to Ann Todd Baum who researched the various facets of Georg Gaertner's career; to Special Agent William Trible of the FBI who provided valuable insights into the psychology of a fugitive and on the inner workings of a federal manhunt; and to Ron Orth, an expert on German militaria, for detailed information on Gaertner's military years. I also wish to thank Barbara A. Frybert who transcribed endless hours of taped interviews and telephone conversations, and Carole Knapp who typed the manuscript.

My deepest gratitude goes to those who provided me with moral support and offered stylistic suggestions throughout. Dr. Candida Lutes, Andrea Elbert, Mary Flori, DVM; Fredrick Warman, Kimberly Ann Sims, and Gina Petruzzelli, R.N. My greatest debt, however, is to Mrs. Traute Manning, in Chicago, a lifetime friend, who provided sound advice and emotional sustenance in endless measure.

INTRODUCTION

This story begins with a late evening telephone call. "Is this Professor Arnold Krammer?" "Yes," I answered cautiously. "The professor who wrote the book called *Nazi Prisoners of War in America*?" I replied that I was he. The caller had a soft voice with the slightest hint of an accent. "Great," he said enthusiastically. "I'm calling to tell you how much I enjoyed reading your book. It's really terrific." I began to warm to the conversation despite the late hour. Everybody loves praise and perhaps no one more than authors. We write for an unseen audience. Almost every profession and trade can see the immediate results of their work: the person on the conveyor belt knows at the end of the day how many bolts were tightened; the physician can watch his patients respond to treatment; the pilot can count the miles flown. Authors seldom meet their readers.

He introduced himself as Dennis Whiles. "Not only is it a fine book," he continued, "but it is absolutely accurate. It's just the way I remember things." Now my ears perked up.

"Oh? I take it that you were once a German prisoner of war in the United States?" I asked. Most of the half a million German POWs here during the war had a wonderful time, and, after their repatriation in 1945, thousands returned from Europe at the first opportunity. I've interviewed them by the score.

"Yes," he mumbled, "I was."

Now I was getting really curious. He was clearly calling long distance and the periodic interruption by the operator who requested "eighty-five cents for the next three minutes, please," indicated that he was calling from a phone booth as well.

For the next ten or fifteen minutes we chatted about his experiences as a POW. One story quickly led to another, and I got the feeling that he had not shared these experiences in many years, if ever. Recollections and anecdotes came tumbling out: the impish pranks they played on each other and on the guards, the loneliness, their makeshift hobbies, and their anxieties about the war and the safety of their loved ones in Germany. Dennis recalled the humorous moments, such as the time some fellow POWs at Camp Deming, New Mexico, brewed up a batch of moonshine and hid the contraband in the altar of the camp chapel, and the frightening times when small cliques of hardened Nazis roamed the camp bullying and threatening those less committed to Hitler's cause. His recollections spanned more than two years as a German prisoner of war in America.

It was nearing midnight. I had a pile of work to finish and gently began to close down our conversation. "Perhaps we can continue another time," I suggested. Dennis started to get flustered. He was caught up in events that took place more than forty years before and was understandably reluctant to halt in midstream. Still, it was time for me to get back to work. I thanked Dennis for taking the time to call and for sharing his wartime experiences with me. He suddenly blurted out that this was not just an ordinary call by a former POW to reminisce about the old days with the historian of that era.

"This is a very emotional moment for me," he said in a whisper.

"Oh?" For a full ten seconds neither of us spoke a word as I waited for him to compose his thoughts. I couldn't imagine what he was trying to say but the tension was palpable.

Finally he cleared his throat and said softly: "I am the last fugitive German prisoner of war. I escaped from Camp Deming, New Mexico, in 1945 and have been on the run for forty years. I want to come in from the cold."

I was dumbfounded. One of the fascinating epilogues of the POW experience is the story of the handful of Germans who successfully escaped captivity. The FBI tracked them down over the next decades. Two were arrested in 1953, another in 1954, one in 1959, and one in 1964. Since 1964 a single German fugitive remained at large: a former sergeant in Rommel's Afrika Korps named Georg Gaertner whose story I had described in my book. My late-night caller had to be he.

"Hello, Mr. Gaertner," I said warmly.

He laughed and said softly, "Hello, Professor Krammer."

The following book is his story.

Arnold Krammer

HITLER'S
LAST SOLDIER
IN AMERICA

ONE

I T WAS THE eeriest scene you can imagine: a vast empty scrubland bathed in stark white moonlight; the desert stretched endlessly in every direction. It looked ghoulish and it was very cold. And absolutely still. There was nothing out there and yet, as I lay on the ground panting and sweating with fear, the sounds of the insects and distant coyotes seemed deafening. I kept praying that no one had spotted me. "Please, God, don't let the searchlights find me." I waited for the sentries, rifles on their shoulders, to pass. If they saw me I was dead. I held my breath and lay motionless in the moonlight. They passed only a couple of yards away and continued along the length of the parallel rows of barbed wire fences. I was almost free. Sharply etched in black in the middle of the desert was a large prison camp: long rows of squat barracks, surrounded by huge guard towers, armed sentries, and miles of barbed-wire fences. The camp held more than 600 inmates and I had been one of them. It wasn't a prison for Americans, even though it was only 50 miles outside Lordsburg, New Mexico. We were all German soldiers—part of the more than 425,000 of us who were captured in North Africa and Europe and brought to America in captivity. I was a sergeant in Rommel's Afrika Korps and had planned this escape for weeks. The moment had arrived, and my life now hung in the balance. "Please, God. Don't let them see me." I inched away from the fence, farther and farther. A searchlight swept terrifyingly close, and I froze until it went by. So far, so good. A few more yards. Wild-eyed, I rose to a crouch and moved stealthily into the desert. No shots. I began to think that I might make it. When I finally dared to look back, I was startled to see the prison camp almost half a mile in the distance, the searchlights moving along the perimeter of the silent dark complex. They hadn't seen me after all. I paused to catch my breath, double-checked my direction toward the distant freight train on the horizon, and began to run for my life. After more than two decades in Weimar Germany and Nazi Germany, months on the battlefields of North Africa, and two years in American prisoner-of-war camps, I was finally and gloriously free. I was twenty-four-years old.

FORTY YEARS HAVE passed since World War II, and I can still remember the moment I escaped from the prisoner-of-war camp. Whenever I let my mind drift to that September night in 1945, I can visualize every scene unfolding like a slow-motion movie. For weeks I had been planning my escape from the prison camp, pacing off the perimeter of the camp grounds, and estimating distances between the long rows of tarpaper barracks and the guard towers, between the sentry boxes and the barbed-wire fences. To any of the other six hundred German combat veterans in Camp Deming, in a remote southwestern corner of New Mexico, I was simply *Unteroffizier K.O.B.* (Kriegstoffizierbewerber) Georg Gaertner. My POW number was 81G–80392, and I lived in Barracks 614. I had been captured on April 13, 1943, during the battle for Tunis, and shipped, with thousands of other prisoners, to the prison camps in the United States. Nearly half a million of us "Nazis," captured on the battlefields of North Africa and Europe, spent the remainder of the war years in America. We brought in the harvests, worked in the factories, and maintained the military posts. It still astonishes me that most Americans today don't even realize that we were here.

The photograph that appeared on FBI wanted posters in government buildings and post offices for nearly forty years shows a tall, rangy, rural kid, a bit weather-beaten around the eyes from months of squinting in the scorching sun of North Africa. There was also a look of weariness and sadness—almost a haunted stare; the eyes of a kid who had seen too much of life too quickly. Yet, at the same time (and, perhaps, I am the only one who can really tell), there is an impishness there as well, a twinkle for a new adventure. Add to that face a pair of wide ears (which I spent most of my childhood lamenting) and a rather long, prominent nose (which my mother called "noble"), and you have the young Georg Gaertner. Every now and again over the past forty years, I have daringly strolled near my own wanted poster on a post office wall for a quick glance of reacquaintance with my youth. The poster was always real enough, however, as was the fact that I was (am) a federal fugitive. I am an escaped German prisoner of war, and have been hunted by the FBI, U.S. Army security, immigration, and every local police force in the country. I have often speculated on the fact that any person who walked through a post office or VA building or tax department—any government bureau with a bulletin board—could be the one to take away my freedom. Someone walking toward me might recall the wanted poster as our eyes met. Any passing acquaintance in life could recognize my picture months or years later and call the police. The cop who stopped me for speeding or who simply pulled alongside me at a red light could be the one to put me in the penitentiary. Arrest was always moments away.

When the war ended and all 425,000 German prisoners were shipped out, the War Department was unable to account for only twelve prisoners. I was one of them.

I have remained at large until the publication of this book, nearly forty years; no other German POW has been a fugitive longer. My odyssey began that September in Camp Deming, New Mexico.

ESCAPES AMONG THE prisoners of war were not uncommon. As POWs, we all had heard stories about our comrades who had somehow managed to break out. The camp rumor mills often relayed exciting tales about one of our boys (we always solemnly concluded with admiration that he must have been an Afrika Korps man), who had made a daring escape through an elaborate tunnel or who audaciously strolled through the main gate wearing a camp-made replica of an American uniform. We whistled in admiration when we heard about someone who had pole-vaulted over the double fence from an adjacent barracks roof, or slipped out hanging beneath a truck. We even grudgingly commended the unimaginative majority who simply walked away from their lightly guarded work parties that were contracted out to local farmers. Everyone knew someone who was collecting equipment for a possible escape: an Esso map swiped from the glove compartment of an army jeep; a pair of stolen pliers; a few hidden dollars, illegal to POWs, for a possible bribe to a guard.

Some of the boys, and that's really what we were, thought of little else. Their motives differed, however. There were those who just had "cabin fever" and talked incessantly about what they would do on the outside, the cities they would see, and the girls they would meet. The professional military men (nobody I knew) considered it their patriotic duty to escape, as did a small, secretive group of dyed-in-the-wool Nazis who spent most of their time muttering ominously about taking our names for punishment after Germany won the war. These men we avoided, as much because of their boring political tirades as by the nagging fear that they might turn to vigilante "justice" if they got the opportunity. Most of us were simply nonpolitical and grateful to be out of the war. We were determined to make the best of a bad situation. Food was certainly better here than in the German army, and we had a wide variety of distractions: PX-canteen, newspapers, concerts and plays put on by the men, and correspondence courses through local universities. I even played in the tennis championships at one camp. Sometimes, we had wine and beer in the PX-canteen, and we ate meat dishes three days a week while the rest of America was rationed and counting up Red Meat Points. No wonder most of the local communities dourly referred to their nearby POW camps as "The Fritz Ritz"! Hell, under those conditions you couldn't drive most of the men out of those camps.

Still, it was far from a rosy life. We were in a prison, after all. However comfortable, we were in a strange and hostile country, thousands of miles from our homes and families. True, we were out of the war and in the relatively gentle care of the United States. Our safety was insured by both the Geneva Convention of 1929 and by Washington's anxious commitment to our comfort as the best assurance of similar treatment by the German government toward the 90,000 American POWs in its hands. But, if I had to reduce our lives as prisoners of war at Camp Deming, to, say, three basic problems, they would be: the scorching heat and an occasional chance meeting with a New Mexican rattlesnake; a potential brush with the Nazis and unbowed militarists in our midst; and *boredom*. I know it must seem hard to believe that with all the diversions available to us (not to mention the many social activities and crafts programs provided to us by the YMCA and the Catholic Welfare Agency), boredom was our biggest problem. Much of our day was spent in idle chatter and aimless strolls. Remember that I was a POW for more than two years! The boredom was compounded by our isolation. The war was remote (Thank God!) and most of the war news was depressing for us. We had little contact with our American guards, not the cream of the crop anyway, and few of us had ever seen our camp commandants—Capt. Daniel J. Smith, Lt. John A. Doyle, and Lt. Seymour Geller—who came and left.

We lived a standard military routine. Up at 6:30 A.M., breakfast of oatmeal and coffee between 7:00 and 8:00, then off to our assignments. Most of us at Deming worked at maintenance jobs around the camp or as clerks at the nearby Army Air Force base. At other camps, especially those closer to civilization, POWs were contracted out to labor-starved farmers or as assembly-line workers in local factories. I heard about one bunch of POWs who spent the war years, ironically, as Kosher meatpackers in Farmington, New Jersey. Moreover, we were paid 80 cents a day in the canteen coupons in lieu of U.S. currency. Eighty cents a day doesn't sound like much today, but in those days it bought eight packs of cigarettes or eight beers! My jobs ranged from a clerk-typist in the administration building to my job at the time of my escape as draftsman at the Post Engineer's office. Most often, however, the fact that I had studied English before the war (what a fortuitous decision), made me the unofficial camp translator. I was often called upon to interpret the commandant's occasional instructions to the POWs or a War Department memo posted on our camp bulletin board. Our routine was broken by a lunch of bologna sandwiches, then back to our petty tasks until late afternoon. The rest of our day was spent socializing/conspiring/pursuing hobbies/writing letters. Dinner in the large mess-barracks usually consisted of spaghetti, chipped beef on toast ("SOS" familiar to any military man), or corned beef hash, milk and coffee, followed by pudding or locally available fruit. Evenings were spent playing dominoes or cards in the PX-canteen. It sounds like a restful schedule, I'll admit, but as the weeks turned into months, and the months years, time became a heavy burden. Yet, like most of the prisoners who endured the same mind-numbing existence, I was resigned to the situation and tried to make the best of it. Life behind the wire was boring, God knows, but tolerable. I had no serious interest in escaping.

Besides, where would I go? When my ship arrived at Norfolk, Virginia, from the holding pens in North Africa, I was transported by train to my new home. For the first time I realized how vast America was. Europeans had no concept of such distances. The impressions of the United States held by most Germans, including Hitler, were formed by the adolescent novels of Karl May. He wrote dozens of wildly popular books about the old West—frothy novels like *Old Shatterhand* and *Old Winneteu*—without ever having been in America. Generations of us learned about a mythical United States from those little potboilers. Far from being a distant frontier, sparsely populated by pioneer families and noble Red Men, America, as we learned to our astonishment from the windows of our POW trooptrain, was sophisticated, industrial, and almost endless. It took nearly ten days to reach my first destination at Camp McLean, Texas. America was startlingly large, and I had long ago shrugged off any serious thoughts of getting back to Germany on my own.

Moreover, a POW who tried to escape was taking a real chance on being killed. However well planned and imaginative the effort, the man who stepped into the "kill zone" between the two barbed wire fences surrounding the camp risked a burst of machine-gun fire from the high sentry towers. We were certainly warned often enough: one "*Halt*" from a guard, then he was free to shoot. Furthermore, it was generally accepted knowledge that the bright yellow letters, "PW," stenciled on the front and back of our uniforms and work clothes were to serve as targets. We all heard stories about guards who were particularly trigger-happy—men who had been recently recycled home from combat overseas, or who had been POWs themselves in Germany and were given a "soft" job in the backwater of the war. Whatever the Army's reasoning, these men made particularly dangerous guards. We heard new horror stories about the skittish temperament of the POW guards every time a group of prisoners passed through Camp Deming in transit to some other camp; other stories we read in the newspapers. The following incidents I know to be true. At Camp Concordia, Kansas, for example, a German prisoner was shot to death while trying to retrieve a soccer ball that he had defiantly kicked into the fences; another incident occurred at Fort Knox, Kentucky, when two POWs were killed by a guard who repeatedly warned them to clear the fence area; at Camp Ovid, Colorado, three men were killed by a guard, recently recycled from combat overseas, when they appeared to attack him; and at a branch camp near Parma, Ohio, a guard shot a German POW after he was repeatedly warned to stop singing a song that ridiculed American servicemen. Thus, we were keenly aware that our guards were not to be trifled with.

We were also aware that they were getting more hostile during the closing months of the war. The invading Allied armies revealed the horrible atrocities of the concentration camps and mass extermination centers. Such unspeakable barbarity repelled all civilized men, especially

20

those of us in the Afrika Korps who had spent our military years a continent away from these events. Many of us were sickened that we represented, fought for, a government that would do such things. To our guards, however, we were all simply "Nazis." We were all guilty. (And, for many years, illogically, I felt that I had somehow contributed to those horrors.)

The end of the war also meant that the United States would soon have its captured soldiers back from enemy hands. With their liberation, we all realized, the War Department no longer needed to worry about our comfort. Our treatment in the United States would no longer affect the safety of the American POWs in German hands. We knew it and, to our growing apprehension, we knew that the guards knew it. There was an increasingly unfriendly aura between us, but few POWs considered the risks of escape worthwhile. We'd just stick it out.

We followed the deteriorating course of the war over the radio and through newspapers. Both were made available to us by the American authorities who, to their great credit, worked hard to show us the benefits of democracy and a free society. Most of us had spent our formative adolescent years under the Nazis, and, as basic as an uncensored press may seem to Americans, it was rather strange to us. We had grown up with politics and propaganda. The War Department courageously put democracy into action, perhaps as an experiment with a captive audience or to prepare us for life in postwar Europe, and every camp received subscriptions to *The New York Times* and local state newspapers. Each barrack also received a radio. We were suspicious for months, of course, since we couldn't believe that the United States would allow us to read about such things as union strikes, race riots, and military reversals. To be honest, we started out delighted at the embarrassing articles about labor or food shortages, gangland killings, and of America's blatant discrimination against its black citizens. We were astonished that the government would allow such negative items to reach print, especially during wartime when such information could be used as propaganda by the enemy. Gradually we began to realize that if the government was willing to disclose its failures to the public, then surely the positive items were true as well.

What finally convinced us that we were not being fed propaganda, I believe, was the news of the Battle of the Bulge in December 1944. Every day we followed with fascination the detailed accounts of the savage fighting; the U.S. Army caught off guard and driven back by the last-ditch

21

German offensive; the miscalculations made by both sides; and finally, the disintegration of the *Wehrmacht* and the allied invasion of the Fatherland. Understandably, we went from elation to depression during that last week of 1944 as the ultimate outcome became clear. But, at the same time, we knew the reports were accurate. We also learned that whatever the drawbacks of democracy (and we knew there were many), it represented Truth in Practice. All but the most embittered among us admitted that, given a choice, we would choose democracy with little hesitation. Since I was the unofficial camp translator, it was my responsibility to read the news to the men. That assignment not only helped to perfect my English, but convinced me, perhaps more than the others, about the importance of freedom to the growth of the human spirit. Yet, however noble my thoughts, they were still only thoughts. The danger of escape still outweighed the benefits. Maybe the end of the war would offer me some new options.

On May 2, 1945, we were dumbstruck to learn of Hitler's suicide. Somehow we had grown to believe that *der Fuehrer* was invulnerable. The men reacted as one might expect. Some were despondent; after all, we had been raised to revere him. Others were angry that Hitler would have taken the coward's way out after dragging Germany into a disastrous world war. Most of us, however, were generally saddened, not about Hitler, but about the death of Germany. What would we be returning to when they finally sent us home?

Home was all we could think about now that the war was officially over. We discussed the options endlessly. The rumor mills shifted into high gear, and those "in the know" (usually a clerk for an American officer) produced steady streams of authoritative and ever-changing scenarios. Our dream, of course, was to be shipped back to Germany as soon as possible. While the papers were filled with stories about ruined cities, starvation conditions, and social chaos, Germany was our home. Our families and loved ones were there. But the realities of the situation indicated that an early return home was improbable.

At the end of one late-night's heated discussion, we agreed that we were not going directly back to Germany. Considering the devastation and upheaval, the U.S. Occupation Forces in Germany would not welcome the appearance of more than 400,000 well-fed German combat veterans. Who knew how many unrepentant Nazis were among us (we often wondered ourselves), or how many hard cases who didn't consider themselves bound by the official surrender? There was still talk about a final uprising by Nazi fanatics in the so-called Southern Redoubt. The facts were overwhelming: the War Department wouldn't chance shipping us home at this time. Moreover, we even wondered if American farmers, desperate for workers until the troops came home, would allow the government to ship us anywhere.

Then, at the end of another impassioned late-night discussion, we also came to the opposite conclusion: we would probably not remain in the United States much longer. Our new reasoning was based on the fact that the American public was in an ugly mood regarding Germans. The recent unfolding of the horrors of Auschwitz, Dächau, Büchenwald, Mauthausen, and Belsen made us all appear to be mass murderers. Then the public learned about the shocking massacre of more than seventy American prisoners, hands bound, at Malmédy, Belgium, by an SS unit during the Battle of the Bulge. Grisly news photographs of the unearthed scene enraged the nation further against Germans (though we, as military men, were equally outraged by such barbarism). Reports then began to appear in the papers about the poor treatment received by American POWs held in German camps. Americans were furious that their kindness toward nearly half a million German POWs in the United States was seldom reciprocated by the other side. Returning American POWs disclosed episodes about being marched five hundred miles through snow and rain; of eating cats and fighting over potato peelings; of beatings and other cruelties. In the camp, we found ourselves increasingly shaken by the stupidity and inhumanity of the government we had fought for. We were also growing mildly concerned for our safety. The quality of our camp food deteriorated rapidly, which we attributed to public hostility and the fact that, with the war over, Washington no longer needed to protect U.S. prisoners by "coddling" us. Relations with our camp guards, erratic during the best of times, were becoming ominously tense. Even those guards, often kids themselves, who had befriended the prisoners, were silent and glowering. The newspapers were filled with anti-Nazi tirades, and public interest began to focus on our fate. Union leaders thundered that we were taking jobs from returning vets and that we should be shipped out immediately. Legislation to begin our repatriation was introduced by Representative George Bender of Ohio, Senator Maybank of South Carolina, and Senator McMahon of Connecticut; and the Wisconsin legislature rose as a body to demand our prompt deportation "lest the gainful employment of our citizenry be seriously jeopardized." We watched, transfixed, as our fate was debated in the press. We were horrified to see a reader suggest in *The New York Times* that a shortage of blood plasma be filled by the "systematic bleeding" of the German POWs in the United States! (Don't think that didn't make us squirm.) Clearly, a growing segment of the American public wanted us out as soon as the returning troops came home to pick up the labor slack. But when that might be, or where we would be sent, was still hotly debated. Through the late summer of 1945 we waited with growing anxiety about our fate.

The answer appeared on our camp bulletin board the first week in September. Several dozen men, I remember, crowded around me in the hot morning sun to hear the translation of the War Department announcement. As I plowed through the several paragraphs of "bureaucratese," our future came into focus. The War Department declared that we would not be repatriated directly to Germany (which we had already concluded), nor were we to remain in the United States (which we had also concluded). In a Solomon-like decision, the War Department had found a middle ground. The German prisoners of war were to be shipped to Europe and there turned over to the British and French for use as laborers on postwar reconstruction projects. Groans rippled through the crowd, although we each gave silent thanks that Russia was not mentioned. (The prospect of being shipped to Russia was always our greatest terror; a whispered, and almost primeval fear. Moreover, in light of Washington's frantic efforts to prevent a total rupture of relations with the USSR, a Russian request for our labor might well have been honored. We dared not even think about the treatment of German POWs in Russian hands. A slave labor camp, Siberia, or worse.) OK, so it was to be France and England (England being our immediate choice considering the brutal German occupation of France), and perhaps two more years until we saw home. Some of the milling men were muttering about being no better than slave labor, and the United States being in the slave trade, but most continued to listen in resigned silence. At least we weren't being shipped to Russia!

I continued to translate the next part of the bulletin. In the very near future, the exact date depending on available transportation, all the prisoners in small satellite branch camps (like our Camp Deming) would be funneled to the larger base camps (ours was Camp Lordsburg, New Mexico). From there, the POWs would be taken by train to a port of embarkation where we would be placed aboard any available vessels for shipment to England and France. All 425,000 men. No exceptions.

24

Then my eyes moved down to the final paragraph and I froze! I tried to compose myself and read the sentence that was to soon change my life. After finishing our labor stints in Britain and France, we would be shipped to Germany and returned directly to our hometowns. Several men in the group gasped as they also realized the significance of the directive. Some of our hometowns had fallen under Russian occupation. We were not going to be discharged as a group somewhere in the American Zone in West Germany, as we had always assumed. Those of us from cities now in East Germany were to be turned over to the Soviets (which did indeed happen)—and we all knew what that meant! I barely managed to control my rising panic as I walked numbly back to my barrack. I was being turned over to the Russians: my fate was sealed.

I spent the next several days lying on my bunk, turning the directive over in my mind. There was no question that my city of Schweidnitz, near Leipzig in east Prussia, was many hundreds of miles within the Soviet zone. My camp job, after all, had been to translate the radio and newspaper war reports for the rest of the men. Like people everywhere during the war, we had followed the course of the battles with little colored pins on a large wall map in the PX-canteen. Those of us from east Prussia watched with horror during the winter of 1944 as the tide of red pins swept westward to engulf our homes. Some of us half-heartedly speculated that maybe the Soviets would withdraw to their own borders after the war, but we all knew better. Our homes and families were all but lost. We stopped talking about it, though the ominous fate of our loved ones was never far from our thoughts for the last six months of the war. Now that the War Department had made clear its intentions to send us back to our hometowns, regardless of zone, we thought of little else.

There was no question that I was in real trouble. I was headed for the Soviet zone and God knows what. For the first time, I allowed myself to wonder about the condition of my family in Russian hands. It suddenly occurred to me that my parents and relatives might already be enroute to Siberia; perhaps my father's position with the Reichsbahn railroads had made him suspect, or the fact that I was a soldier in the Afrika Korps had jeopardized their safety. We had corresponded periodically during the war, first from North Africa and later from my camps in America. But no letters had arrived for some time, due, I thought, to the chaos in Germany at the end of the war. But maybe it was more than that; maybe they were prisoners themselves, or worse. My mind raced furiously to consider all the possibilities and weigh my options. Within a matter of days I convinced myself, without another shred of evidence, that my parents and loved ones were lost. I know that it sounds odd—it seems curious to me today. But in retrospect I realize that I had to do it: I had to convince myself that my parents were dead if I was to be free to act on my own. Nothing I did now could hurt them. I had burned my bridges behind me. (I was so sure that they were dead that I nearly fainted some thirty-nine years later when I learned that my parents had not only survived the end of the war but that they had escaped into the American Zone and safety. To my astonishment and no small amount of guilt. I found out that they had lived well into the 1960s, and had passed away without ever giving up hope that I was alive. My picture remained on their dining room table until their deaths.)

In September 1945, however, I was preparing for my only apparent option: escape. Me! The quiet, nonpolitical kid from the sticks, who had not been more than fifty miles from home before I joined the army. Until now, my main interests in life concerned sports and daydreams about girls. My head reeled at the prospect of the danger and adventure that awaited me. For the first time in my life, I was about to take charge of my future.

The fact is that I was fed up with being told what to do. My childhood was typically German: Every member of the family knew what was expected, and our lives were regulated by tradition, habit, local public pressure, religion, and, after the Nazis took power in 1933, by the whims of a dictator as well. School was yet another model of order and discipline. The more I thought about it, the more I was determined to break free of it all and choose my own direction. I had always been told what to do, by my parents, teachers, priests, sports coaches, employers—everyone. What was not controlled by my family and teachers, was regulated by the stifling German bureaucracy. It was a force that Americans simply cannot imagine. Every item and event in your life required a form, tax stamp, signature, or passbook. School diplomas or wedding certificates weren't valid unless they had a little tax stamp in the corner. Permits were required for just about everything, and they had files on everyone. That was one of the ways the Nazis took over so quickly: they simply took control of the bureaucracy.

Then came the army, and anyone who has been in the military knows what that means! The military runs on orders, discipline, and, in my opinion, mindless routine. We Germans have made militarism a national obsession, and the Nazis turned us into robots. The cutting edge, of course, was the German army—the *Wehrmacht*. It elevated discipline to a high art. Isn't that the stereotype of Germans? And frankly, it's not an unjustified image. Discipline has historically been the source of our greatest accomplishments and our most dismal failures. I've always found it ironic that we Germans are at the same time both aggressive and passive, dictatorial and humane; what Goethe called "two souls in one breast." Winston Churchill put it more dramatically: "The Germans are either at your feet or at your throat." I think there is something to that. The same country that produced Goethe, Fichte, Schopenhauer, the world's greatest philosophers, poets, and musicians, also produced Bormann, Himmler, Goering, Heydrich, and the rest of that gang. (Fortunately, since we lost the war, we can blame Hitler on the Austrians.) Anyway, it was the latter group who were in control as I grew up. I was a product of Discipline and Order. And after three years in the *Wehrmacht* and another two in American POW camps, I decided that I had had enough! No one was going to tell me what to do again. I was twenty-four, after all, and wanted to travel, meet girls, play sports, and meet girls. And where better to find that independence than in America? We'd been lectured to death about the virtues of democracy; it was time to see for myself.

I took stock of my survival skills: I was young and in pretty good health; I spoke English reasonably well; and while I had an accent, so did millions of American immigrants. I could teach skiing or tennis, having been a local champion in my youth. I was a good listener and got along well with everybody. Having been an apprentice draftsman as a schoolboy, I had an eye for detail and an awareness of distance. Both skills would be useful in avoiding traps or locating exits. Perhaps most importantly, I had the kind of face that would be overlooked in a crowd. I looked like any tall, skinny farm kid in America. After evaluating my skills and traits, I felt a momentary surge of confidence: I could make it. America, here I come!

Suddenly, there was purpose in my life. I was full of anticipation and the realization that only two barbed-wire fences separated me from my new life. But first came the hard part: I had to escape. Moreover, I had to be successful the first time. There would be no second chance. Any misstep or plain bad luck would bring a barrage of bullets from the already trigger-happy sentries. If the sentries didn't shoot me, I would be thrown in the camp stockade until it was time to ship me to East Germany. No matter how I looked at it, I had to break out of camp, I had to do it soon, and I had to do it right the first time.

Plans raced through my mind. I quickly eliminated the complicated schemes since I had not accumulated the necessary escape items: maps, tools, money, or counterfeit social security or draft card (usually typed on a camp typewriter while an American officer was on his coffee break). Truthfully, I wasn't even sure how far Camp Deming was from anywhere. How naive I was then! My next decision was that I had to escape solo. If no one else knew my plan, no one could give me away, accidentally or otherwise. But how was I going to escape? Tunneling was out since there wasn't enough time or tools. I considered smuggling myself out in a civilian laundry or food truck, but I didn't know their schedules. No. Given the circumstances, the only way was to simply find a shadowy spot along the fence, wait for the right moment, and slip out under the wire. Then it would be a mad dash across the open desert scrubland to safety, wherever that was. There was my entire brilliant plan: simple, solo, and, to continue the alliteration, stupid. It was dumb enough to work, I prayed, and began wandering around the camp in search of that ideal shadowy spot near the fence.

Early in September, I had two great strokes of unexpected luck. The first came when my blue work fatigues came back from the camp laundry without the normally stenciled bright-yellow letters: "PW." I never heard of that happening before, and offered silent thanks to the anonymous screw-up in every system. My original plan (what little there was) called for turning my stenciled work clothes inside out, until I could swipe something off a clothesline; now I stood a far better chance of slipping into the American mainstream unnoticed. FBI posters later claimed that I had escaped in a stolen U.S. Army uniform (with Second Air Force insignia, to be precise), which has irritated me to this day. It not only made me nervous about being charged with some sort of additional crime, but, frankly, it hurt my pride.

My second good fortune came as I was strolling around the camp, lost in a rising panic that each passing day was bringing me closer to learning Russian. I bumped into a group of men who were pointing to something off in the distance. I ambled over as they were discussing a far-off shiny glint moving on the horizon. It was a *train*! I couldn't believe it; why had I never noticed that distant reflection before? I tried to look nonchalant as I tossed the men an airy salute and moved on, but I could barely control my excitement. First the unmarked work clothes, and now, just a few days later, I found that a train passed four or five miles from the camp.

The train now became my main obsession. I had to estimate its distance and figure out the schedule. My spirits soared as I felt success within my grasp. I immediately shifted my daily activities to the area of the camp closest to the railroad line, and I created every imaginable reason that would enable me to stare off in that direction. I became an early-morning bird-watching enthusiast; at noon I sat cross-legged in meditation; and during the afternoon I set up my makeshift easel and painted watercolors of the desert landscape. (I remember being offered a pack of cigarettes for one of my better efforts, a princely sum in camp currency. Smugness aside, the sale gave me an excuse to remain near the fence for another hour, painting one more). It took me about ten days of this kind of activity to work out an accurate train schedule, and to my great relief, I confirmed that one train passed the camp every other day at ten o'clock at night. Talk about luck!

In fact, the whole escape was beginning to take on an almost mystic quality, as though it was somehow predestined. The clothes, the train, my knowledge of English—everything pointed to success. Even today, forty years later, I believe my escape was preordained. I was meant to change my life in America. (Considering that everything had fallen into place within four weeks of my decision to escape, I sometimes laughingly wonder what I could have accomplished if I had begun planning earlier. Given a year, I'll bet that I could have led the entire camp in a mass escape to freedom.)

By September 20, 1945, I decided that I was as ready as I'd ever be. There was nothing to be gained by waiting. Indeed, the longer I waited, the greater the chances that something could go wrong: a change in the train schedule or the discovery of my hidden work clothes; our repatriation process to Europe might suddenly begin; or I might "chicken out" and take my chances with the Russians.

There was an additional reason for moving quickly. I wanted to take advantage of the immediate postwar chaos. Millions of GIs were being demobilized and crowding the nation's train stations and bus depots. Factories were retooling for peacetime production, and the labor force was changing madly to keep pace, a perfect opportunity for the appearance of a nondescript skilled worker. Moreover, I also concluded that the end of the war meant the end of ID cards, security checks, ration books, and amateur spy catchers. The country was heady with victory and the population caught in a maelstrom of movement. The longer I waited, the less my chances of slipping unnoticed into the general population.

Given all these facts, and the feeling that Fate was somehow presenting me with this single opportunity to save myself and begin life anew. I decided to throw the dice and escape the very next night: September 21, 1945. All I would take along would be my small shaving kit and a silver ring I had bought from an Arab in North Africa. The inlaid emblem on the ring was perfect: it was a running antelope. I remember lying awake most of that night, going over and over the plan, and vowing, rather melodramatically, that the next night would see me free, enslaved, or dead. I went through the next day in a sweaty daze. I loitered around the barracks near the fence and made furious mental notes for my dash in the dark. I calculated and re-calculated the time I needed to reach the train as it moved slowly past Camp Deming. If I bolted too early, a surprise head-count back in camp would find me missing and easily caught out in the flat scrubland. Five minutes too late and I would watch the train disappear in the distance. I gave myself thirty minutes to crawl under the double set of barbed wire and thirty minutes more to race the several miles to the train. One hour! According to my calculations, the train passed at 10:00 P.M.—I would escape at 9:00 while the men were watching the weekly movie.

By dinner time I was a nervous wreck. I was sure that every passing glance carried a knowing wink and every greeting a surreptitious "good luck." With so many well-wishers, I convinced myself, how could I back out now?

At the stroke of 9:00 P.M., while all the other men were jeering at a "B" Western movie in the camp mess hall, I slipped out of my barracks into the night. To my astonishment, I found myself not in a protective blanket of darkness, as I had expected, but in the midst of a moonlit scene bright enough to read a newspaper by. I cursed my stupidity at overlooking the possibility of a full moon but went ahead. Scampering across the camp, I made it safely to the darkened corner of a barrack nearest to the wire fence. I stood in the shadows for several minutes, my heart pounding, as I watched the ominous sweeps of the searchlights over the silent prison camp. Back and forth down the length of the fence, then slowly the beams moved back past me to the other end. All the way down, then back; down, then back; and as the searchlight went past me the next time, I stepped out of the shadow. Crouched over, I ran to the first fence. There was no turning back now. If a sentry spotted me, I could be shot. And if I ran back to the shadow and a sentry saw me, I could be shot as well. Nearly wild-eyed with fear, I scooted under the bottom strands of barbed wire, never noticing the cuts and scratches. Now I was in the so-called "kill zone" between the fences, barely able to control my panic.

I forced myself to lie quietly next to the outer fence, hoping that the sound of my heart couldn't be heard all the way up into the guard tower. "God, how could they not know I'm here?" For a few seconds, I even considered the possibility that they were all watching my torture, and when I made it under the last fence, the searchlights would rivet on me—and *bang*! I can still feel that exact moment: lying next to the last fence, face pushed into the sandy soil, in bright moonlight, with the sentry's beam probing relentlessly down the "kill zone" toward me. Except for the sounds of the crickets and the muffled distant laughter from the movie barrack, the world around me was absolutely silent. As I huddled at the base of the fence, almost paralyzed, the searchlight was moving inexorably toward me. Now! I mustered every ounce of reserve strength, lifted the lower strands of the barbed wire, and rolled under and out. No gunfire yet. I paused to catch my breath and clawed at my watch to see if I still had a chance to reach the train. According to the plan, I had only one hour to accomplish the whole escape, and I knew I had used up most of the time getting through the wire. I prayed I still had a few minutes left. As my watch came into view, I couldn't believe my eyes! It was only 9:11! What I thought had been an eternity had lasted only eleven minutes. I could make it after all. I took a deep breath and inched away from the camp perimeter into the stark, black-and-white lunar landscape of the New Mexican desert.

It was an eerie, surrealistic scene. A bright moonlit tableau dotted with countless, small, black desert bushes. Between them were tall cactus plants, like menacing sentinels, silhouetted every few hundred yards. At first, I crept slowly away from the camp, still expecting a sudden shout of alarm followed by a hailstorm of bullets. I stopped to catch my breath and paused to look back. The full moon made the camp appear almost otherworldly, like science fiction. The fences and the rows of military barracks were starkly outlined in the ghostly bright light, the searchlights moving relentlessly around the prison camp. Perhaps the most striking thing was the almost-total silence; hardly a sound but the desert wind. I remember smiling to myself at the uniqueness of the quiet after so many years of living with large numbers of shouting, singing, and snoring men. I thought to myself: "I'm going to love freedom."

When I felt I was out of earshot of the camp guards, I rose to a crouch and broke into a trot. After a few hundred yards, and a sudden swerve around a startled and irritated rattlesnake, I ran toward the railroad tracks like a jackrabbit.

Now I was getting confident. Somehow I was going to pull this off. Me! Georg Gaertner from the rural hamlet of Schweidnitz; formerly a soldier in war-torn North Africa, and more recently, a guest of the U.S. War Department. I enjoyed the sound of the word "formerly"—it carried the feeling of past tense and the promise of a new beginning. Not that I was out of the woods, I reminded myself. In fact, this might have been the easiest part. I still had to get to the tracks, jump aboard a moving train undetected, and survive an indeterminate journey to an unknown destination. There was no way of knowing where the train was going, but it didn't really matter: I had not chosen a final destination in any case. (Beyond the immediacy of escape, I had only toyed with a woolly plan to work my way to the safety of a pro-German country in South America, perhaps Argentina or Paraguay. From there, my fantasy was to sneak aboard a ship bound for Germany and return to a hero's welcome.) I decided simply to stay as flexible as possible.

Suddenly, I stumbled onto the railroad tracks. Panting furiously, I checked my watch to find that it would be fifteen minutes until the train arrived. I paced around to catch my breath and to stay warm in the chilly night air. Where's that damn train? Everything depends on that train! Then I heard the locomotive in the distance! Ten o'clock on the dot. Thank God for the inviolate tradition of railroads the world over: the sacredness of the timetable. For the first time, I saw that the train was a slow-moving freight train, with the words "Southern Pacific" painted across nearly every boxcar. As the locomotive headlight swept the tracks before it, I managed to find some cover so the engineer wouldn't spot me in the stark landscape.

Within minutes the long train was rolling past, just a dozen yards away. Every few cars had an open sliding door, and I poised myself for a likely prospect. I saw one moving toward me, the door wide open. Coiled like a spring, I counted to three, and lunged. I ran alongside the rattling train, grabbed the moving door frame, and heaved myself into the open boxcar. I made it! Without even thinking, I scampered across the dirty wooden plank floor to the furthest dark corner and hid in the shadows. Was I alone? Maybe I had stumbled into a nest of thieves or murderers who might rob me and leave me for dead. God, for a moment I longed for the safety of the POW camp. My eyes darted from corner to corner: nobody. I was alone after all. I rolled the heavy door shut and settled into a corner. I was terribly cold and getting hungry. All I could do was cover myself with several armfuls of smelly straw to keep warm, and wonder where I would end up. The whole escape, from beginning to end, had taken one hour! It was the most important hour in my life. At nine o'clock I was a prisoner, and at ten o'clock I was free. *Free!* I liked the sound of that. I huddled back in the corner, my future completely uncertain, and broke into a wide smile. I was free! I was free!

TWO

THE JOURNEY LASTED three desperately hungry days. Unbelievably, I had embarked on my escape without ever considering the need for extra food. It had somehow just never occurred to me. But there I was: huddled in the dark corner of a dirty boxcar, covered with straw to keep warm, without food or water, on an unknown odyssey. My moods changed with the passing hours. For a while I would be optimistic, almost euphoric. I had finally escaped, though my success was due more to blind luck than planning. Still, I had done it. Then, suddenly, the reality of my situation would settle over me like a pall. What had I accomplished! I left a safe, warm, protected environment where I was reasonably well-fed and surrounded by my comrades, for who-knows-what. Now I was an "Escaped Nazi" who would soon be the object of a nationwide manhunt. My picture would be everywhere. If I had been an escaped Allied POW in Germany, I could be shot by the authorities; I expected no less in the United States. In fact, it was not only the authorities I would have to fear. I was at the mercy of any hostile citizen; someone, perhaps, who had lost a brother or father overseas. Maybe I would be spotted by a former combat veteran who might react violently by instinct. For that matter, here I was, vulnerable to any hobo or thug riding the rails, or to a harsh railroad detective. I was helpless in the face of any injustice or crime. I had no friends, no money. I couldn't even turn to the police for aid. Gradually my panic would subside and I would grow confident again. Then the cycle would start all over again.

After a while I began to doze. The rhythm of the train wheels on the rails, hour after hour, lulled me into long periods of restless sleep. My mind began to drift to my childhood, my hometown of Schweidnitz in Silesia, and the events that brought me to this endless train ride. For the last time in my life, I dreamt of Germany.

WHEN HITLER CAME to power in 1933, the country was electrified by the possibility of sweeping change. The Nazis claimed to have a solution to the political chaos of the Weimar Republic years of the 1920s and the crippling depression that followed. Germany was willing to embark on almost any new path, provided it brought economic relief, steady employment, and some semblance of restored national pride. Nearly a quarter of the population of Germany, most unemployed and ready to believe any bombastic promises, went to the polls in November 1932, and made their compact with the Devil.

The changes we brought on ourselves—though I was only twelve years old at the time—were more radical and swift than anyone had thought possible. Within months, trade unions were dissolved, opposition political parties driven underground, minorities purged from the professions, and working women encouraged to leave the marketplace for the Victorian ideals of Motherhood. Consequently, the promised jobs became more plentiful. Moreover, the new regime embarked on a massive and highly publicized nationwide program of industrial recovery: new highways crisscrossed Germany, the great steel mills of the Ruhr were back in full operation, and singing men marched to bring in the harvests. Whether pleased or displeased with the results of their choice, Germans realized that they had a tiger by the tail.

Rural towns, however, changed the least. There were some open-air party rallies, some swastika flags about, the occasional appearance of a preening government official, and whispered gossip about the roundup of Jews in a distant larger city—but little else to indicate the awesome changes that were occurring outside of the district. Like farmers anywhere, rural Germans knew that real stability rested on the traditional values of piety, family, patriotism, hard work, and the inevitable change of the seasons. That was the basis of life in the mid-eastern farming community of Schweidnitz, where I was born on December 18, 1920.

Schweidnitz began as a medieval trading town that traced its heritage and much of its architecture back to the twelfth century. It was tucked in

36

the sweeping agricultural valley that stretched eastward from Breslau, the provincial capital, to the gentle Eulengebirge (Owl Mountains) and the broad Oder Plain. It was a town of gingerbread houses and wide cobblestone streets, parks and skating rinks, and a statue of Frederick the Great in the middle of the town square. By the mid-1930s, the farming community of Schweidnitz could boast almost 35,000 inhabitants and our own town orchestra.

The Gaertner family lived in town; we were not farmers. Our family was comfortably middle class, the very picture of the traditional German family. My father, Paul, was a trainmaster for the *Deutsches Reichsbahn,* a position of some substance: a government official. A family portrait, circa 1940, says everything. Seated are my parents in their formal attire: Paul: bald, large girth, unsmiling; and my mother, Emma, a matronly Victorian woman with a tiara and a soft, warm smile. Behind them stand their three grown children. Young Paul was then twenty-nine, quiet and poetic. Lotte was twenty-four and an image of our matronly mother. Lastly, a tall, skinny lad with a long nose and wide ears: me. The only item missing might be a picture of the old field marshal, von Hindenburg, which did, in fact, hang prominently in our family living room. It was a household where the parents doted on their children.

Papa owned the three-story apartment building at 9 Glubrechstrasse, and our family lived on the ground floor. His hobby was his pigeon coop in the small backyard, and Mama's domain was the kitchen. Next door was a small park, the Volksgarten, where popularly attended concerts and occasional Nazi party rallies were held. Church attendance was taken for granted, and there was no discernible friction between the Catholic half of the community, which included us, and the Protestants. Education was adequate but not overdone; sports and a reverence for Prussian military tradition took precedence. Life in Schweidnitz was as predictable as the seasons.

As in most European households of the era, it was Mama who raised the family and maintained general order. When I think back to my childhood, I see my mother smiling patiently while I learned to ice skate at the local outdoor rink, or playing in the Richthofen Memorial Park (Baron Manfred von Richthofen, the World War I flying ace, was born in Schweidnitz), or while I sat eating ice cream under the striped awning of the Kaiser Café. Papa was often gone for days or weeks on railroad business, sometimes as far away as Breslau, returning with armloads of gifts, knicknacks for the house, and stylish woolen clothes for the severe Silesian winters. On balance, my childhood was regulated, uneventful, and rather lonely.

Salvation came in the form of my boyhood friends: Horst Trispel, handsome, bright, outgoing; Heinz Suchan, the comedian among us; and Ursula von Muller, a coy, aristocratic little girl whom we all loved in vain. We were an inseparable quartet until World War II took us each in different directions. Together we went skiing in the Eulengebirge mountains, counted railroad cars along the train tracks, and played cowboys and Indians like our heroes in Karl May's romantic novels about the American wild west. It was Horst, Heinz, Ursula, and I. When we reached our teenage years, we boys got into mischief on our own, roaring through local villages on a DKW motorcycle, stalking crows with an air rifle, and planning daredevil stunts to impress our Ursula.

School was far less exciting. At the age of fourteen, after we finished grammar school, we all took a test to determine which of two programs we should pursue. The two programs were taught at two separate schools, which were located on either side of a large soccer field. One was the Gymnasium Schule, which offered Latin and generally produced doctors and lawyers. On the other side of the soccer field was the Oberreal Schule, more of a technical school, with emphasis on math and engineering. To my parents' delight, my test score was high enough to choose either school. It was an easy decision: Hans and Horst were both going to the Oberreal Schule. Thus, so would I. We enrolled like comrades going off to war. And what a great time we had. The first two years (of four) were spent in philosophical discussions, all-night study sessions, and occasional high-jinks that landed one or all of us in the rector's office for a stern lecture. I majored in architecture, a love I developed walking endlessly through the gingerbread streets of Schweidnitz, and English, which I first learned by reading the foreign newspapers while waiting for my father at the train station.

My real passion, however, was sports. Like everywhere in Europe, soccer was the most popular pastime, and, immodestly, I must admit that I was a terrific player. During the first year at school, I also discovered a new sport: tennis. My father had bought me a violin, which I hated, and at the first opportunity when he left on a trip, I traded the violin to a gullible kid at our rival school, the Gymnasium, for an old tennis racket. Now this was more like it! Good hard exercise and plenty of competition. More importantly, girls came to watch tennis players, not violinists. Somehow my father never noticed that I no longer practiced the violin, any more than he noticed, frankly, when I won the Schweidnitz Junior Tennis Championship, or the Schweidnitz Slalom Skiing Championship. I learned to derive my enjoyment from winning the tournaments rather than from parental enthusiasm over my successes. In a way, it worked out for the best, since it prepared me to live perfectly well without emotional dependence on others, which stood me in good stead during my years as a fugitive.

Everything was shattered when I was fifteen. I caught diphtheria, a near-fatal disease in those days. My cousin in Berlin, in fact, had died of diphtheria, and I almost followed. Our apartment was immediately quarantined and for several weeks there was serious doubt if I would live to see sixteen. I remember my parents nursed me around the clock, using alcohol baths to lower my raging fever. It was probably only the availability of a new antitoxin serum, derived from horse protein, that saved my life. Months of slow recovery passed before our doctor even realized that the diphtheria had left me with a partially paralyzed leg. That discovery, in turn, led to a program of electric shock treatments that eventually restored my leg to full mobility.

My friends rallied around me, and a day seldom passed that Horst, Heinz, and Ursula didn't stop outside of our quarantined apartment to serenade me and throw flowers through the window. But it was a terribly lonely year.

More than that, my school year was gone. In fact, as I was soon to learn, my entire education was finished. I was resigned to the fact that I couldn't make up the lost school year, and that my chums would graduate before me. Then came a new shock: the Oberreal Schule had changed the curriculum to include proficiency in French, which I simply couldn't learn in the little time left in my school career. I wouldn't be able to graduate at all. My bout with that damned diphtheria killed any hopes I had of finishing school or entering the university or of a future in architecture. It was the catastrophe of my youth. My education was over. I didn't even have the basic requirement now to become an officer in the army. As if to underscore my tragedy, within weeks after my recovery I took a spill on my motorcycle and broke my left elbow. That did it! Just what I needed! Six more weeks of pain and immobility. I was sixteen years old and watching my future go up in smoke. After several weeks of self-pity, I concluded that there was simply nothing I could do. The logical expedient of taking a crash course in French and returning to school just seemed excessively harsh. So, in the time-honored adolescent tradition, I decided that if the establishment didn't want me. I didn't want them. All I could do was put aside my worries and concentrate on rebuilding my fragile health. That meant I could turn full time to my favorite sports, tennis and skiing.

For the next two years I lived for little else. It was a wonderful experience, grueling but euphoric. I pursued both sports with single-minded dedication and moved easily into the championship class. At eighteen, I was the Middle Silesian Tennis Champion. Who would have guessed that my competence in tennis and skiing would someday sustain me in America and that I would become well known in professional circles in both sports. I wonder what some of my later tennis partners, movie stars like Lloyd Bridges and Robert Stack, or tennis greats like Bill Tilden, would say if they knew that I was a fugitive German POW who had learned the sport in Nazi Germany.

Thus passed the years 1938 and 1939. I was so engrossed in regaining my health and in improving my sports skills that I barely noticed the growing inevitability of war. Hitler had been startlingly successful in challenging the Versailles powers: remilitarizing in 1935, peacefully reoccupying the French-controlled Rhineland in 1936, joining with Mussolini to test their weapons in the Spanish Civil War in 1936, absorbing Austria in 1938, and then the Sudetenland the same year. Nazism had also reached out to engulf the distant rural towns, and Schweidnitz was no exception. It somehow just happened. A few weekend rallies, then an occasional parade; before any of us really noticed, the Nazis seemed to be everywhere. By the fall of 1938, we were growing used to troop maneuvers outside of town and soldiers strolling through the parks on weekends. It was curious how quickly everyone adjusted to the strangers in our community, a town where we once prided ourselves on knowing the names of everyone we met. I remember thinking how easily a stranger could melt into the mainstream of even a small city if he didn't do anything that would call attention to himself. Act like everyone else; be flexible, passive, but always alert. Have a cover story ready, but be prepared to bolt if someone shows too much curiosity. Above all, I decided, success was only possible if absolutely no one else knew the secret. Not a soul. The tiniest disclosure to a trusted friend during a weak moment, might, in turn, lead to a remark passed to others. It is almost uncanny in retrospect, but at the age of nineteen, watching strangers walk through the Volksgarten in Schweidnitz, I was already fascinated by the problems that might be encountered by a fugitive in an unfamiliar society. Such concerns, I realized, were hardly realistic in my case; where would I find any adventure in a backwoods town like Schweidnitz?

In fact, life was getting pretty lonely in Schweidnitz. With war around the corner, men were being drafted into the army at such a pace that by September 1939, when Hitler marched into Poland, starting World War II, I found myself in a town of kids and old men. Even Horst Trispel, my best friend, had gone into the military. To everyone's surprise, he had become an officer in a heavy motorized artillery regiment of the *Wehrmacht.* Imagine that! In more contemporary terms, it would be as though one's boyhood friend unexpectedly volunteered for combat duty with the Special Forces or the Airborne Rangers. At least that's how it seemed to us. It also seemed to our little group to be so . . . unnecessarily military. But patriotism came even more into fashion with Germany's lightning victories, and more than one normally retiring young man succumbed to the drumbeat of propaganda and the grandeur of a crisp new uniform to answer the call to the colors. Little wonder, then, that Heinz soon announced that he too had enlisted and had been accepted in officers' school in Berlin. I was green with envy, but knew that I stood little chance of being the third musketeer-officer without my Oberreal Schule diploma. (Lord Alfred Tennyson, the nineteenth-century British poet, was profoundly right in stating that the reason men march off to war is because the ladies are watching!) To my surprise, Horst rose to the rank of captain and was decorated in battle. Heinz also became a decorated hero and, rumor had it, later married our Ursula. I tried to stay in touch with Horst and Heinz and our friend Susan Hoffman, but my own adventures prevented me from maintaining contact. I never learned what became of them or even if they survived the war. I would be overjoyed to find out that they had.

Meanwhile, it was already the spring of 1940 and I had not yet been called up for the army. It's true that I was only nineteen years old, but younger boys had already been drafted. I still had a student deferment, but that could not be expected to keep me out for long. My poor health record or the fact that I was the youngest son of the trainmaster seemed likely to delay the inevitable for a little while. I knew that when the time came, however, my relative lack of schooling would destine me for the inglorious enlisted ranks. Yet, whatever the reason and however long my reprieve, I was determined to make the best of my remaining time. I haunted the empty tennis club and the vacant ski lodges in search of almost any ambulatory sports partner and often found myself competing with youngsters and members of the geriatric set. Still and all, I mused, I was one of the few eligible boys left in a town filled with girls, and perhaps if I played my cards right . . . (it didn't help).

By the spring of 1940, I was going squirrelly with boredom and loneliness and decided to find an alternative to the interminable waiting. Suddenly, an opportunity presented itself. I saw an announcement in the newspaper stating that those young men who volunteered for four months of labor service would later be able to choose their branch of military service. Only in Nazi Germany could such a prospect have made sense. Four months of volunteer labor in order to better my chances in the military! On the other hand, what was there to do in Schweidnitz? I was beginning to imagine the hot breath of the draft on my neck and, if military service was inevitable, I figured that I might as well take advantage of every edge. I was keenly aware that I didn't have a high school diploma, and perhaps a four-month stint in the National Labor Service might help me later. So off I went, a front-line soldier in the "Spade Brigade." Several hundred of us from all over the area were shipped to a remote section of East Prussia where we spent the summer draining marshes and digging ditches. It was hard physical labor, but I didn't really mind. I felt that the experience was building up my health and, more importantly, it was keeping the army at arm's length until I could secure the edge I probably needed for future military service. Besides, it was fun. We spent much of our time in shared comradeship: marching, singing, sleeping in pup-tents (and through the indoctrination lectures). In September 1940, my contribution to the Fatherland was finished, and I was shipped back to Schweidnitz to face the music. By the time I returned, both Horst and Heinz were gone.

My secret ambition was to be like Horst Trispel, devastatingly handsome in his officer's uniform, wearing the decorations he won during the Polish offensive in 1939 and in France in 1940. The arrival of a letter from Horst was always a special event, filled with thrilling details of the battles, the heroism of his men, and the soaring joy of direct participation in the events I could only read about in the papers. He often included a small photograph of himself, smiling through the grime of war or surrounded by some comrades or local pretty girls. How the girls chased him, a young Errol Flynn. His most recent letter came from Paris (that dog!) where he was stationed with a motorized artillery unit. There was my answer! My route to heroism was clear: I too would join the artillery. Facilitated by the record of my four-month stint in the National Labor Service. I was accepted without difficulty. After completing the paperwork in October, I was shipped to artillery bootcamp at Ohlau, a godforsaken spot in the bitterly cold tundra some seventy-miles east of Schweidnitz. The moment had finally arrived. I was nineteen years old, a tall gangly kid in my rumpled new uniform, obsessed by fantasies of glory, going off to war.

Whatever dreams I had about leading my brave comrades through shot and shell to victory went out the window as soon as I arrived at bootcamp. I was assigned to a group called the 3rd Heavy Artillery, which turned out to be a decrepit horse-drawn reserve unit leftover from World War I. Hardly what I expected. Worse yet, as a new recruit I was given the illustrious task of shoveling the manure. Every romantic notion I had about the glory of war evaporated as I looked down the long rows of horse stalls, most of which looked as if they hadn't been cleaned out since the war that created my unit. There were hundreds of horses, and they needed to be fed, watered, and groomed daily. After walking down the many rows of aromatic stalls to survey my new domain, I remember spending my first hour—sitting on a large mound of something I dare not think about—like a young recruit in any army, contemplating the joys of military life. Georg, you're in the army now!

Then came my next surprise. The howitzers and artillery pieces were as antiquated as their method of transportation, and while they certainly looked awesome enough from a distance, I had my doubts about their accuracy or safety. For that matter, I wondered if there was sufficient ammunition for them left over from the Great War. To my additional dismay, I soon learned that these lumbering howitzers had to be muscled around by men because the horses were spared for all but the most important parades and troop maneuvers. And woe to the recruit who touched the cannons without wearing gloves during the brutal winter months; he was likely to leave the skin of his hand behind.

Basic training was understandably miserable. Up at dawn, inadequate food, constant marching in the bitter cold, and long hours in the heated aromatic stable; my health was beginning to suffer. One day I simply collapsed. I had pneumonia. The next six weeks were spent in the camp infirmary, and although I was finally warm and comfortable, my unit had completed its training without me. Considering that the same thing had happened to me at school, only then due to diphtheria, I began to wonder if this wasn't developing into a pattern. In any case, I was reassigned to a new unit of recruits coming through basic training and worked hard to finish with them and get out of bootcamp.

No sooner had I been pronounced healthy and joined my new group, than calamity struck again. We were out on a major troop maneuver, covering miles of hilly countryside. We were all on horseback, galloping about, directing the horse-drawn howitzers here and there. At one point we went through a small wooded area and were shunted into a single file along a narrow path. That's when it happened. Something must have frightened the horse in front of me (I never did like horses anyway), and it kicked back and broke my shinbone. Not just fractured, but shattered. I would have gladly traded my bout with either diphtheria or pneumonia for what was to follow. By any account, this was a serious injury, and there was even some talk by the army doctors of amputation! I was given morphine for almost two weeks and would have gladly continued had the doctors not noticed my growing dependence and shifted me to other medication. Yet whatever the medication, my leg simply wouldn't heal. Part of the problem was certainly the severity and complexity of my injury, but part was also due to the lack of skilled doctors (this was the army, after all) and sophisticated medical equipment out in the boondocks of East Prussia. Months passed before I saw the slightest improvement, and it was nearly half a year before I recovered enough to be discharged from the infirmary. My unit and half a dozen more had already graduated from basic training, and I was getting downright embarrassed. Almost a year had passed since I enlisted in October 1940, and I was still in bootcamp. I was a veteran recruit. I was probably more familiar with basic training at Ohlau than anyone there, a fact that did not go unnoticed. In one of the unfathomable ironies for which all armies are notorious, I was promoted to the position of temporary drill instructor! A drill instructor! Considering all the problems I had brought to the Wehrmacht, my bunkmates used to laughingly call me the "Allies' secret weapon." I still smile at the scene: Drill Instructor Gaertner, with his high-pitched bullhorn voice, marching hundreds of men (with the same lowly rank of private) back and forth across the desolate parade ground. That's what I did every day, with the exception of a delightful but brief assignment teaching skiing to several groups of soldiers enroute to the Russian front. I completed my first year in the army. Some adventure! Pneumonia, a still-painful broken shinbone, bad-tempered horses, and constant bitter cold—frankly, I was getting damned tired of the whole thing. It was time to look for an adventure in a warmer climate.

The first break occurred in the spring of 1942. I was selected for Officers' Preparatory School in Heidelberg. I suspect that the authorities at the Ohlau Basic Training Camp were less impressed with my military skill than they were simply anxious to get rid of me. But whatever the reason, here was my opportunity for advancement (with only an Unterabitur diploma) and, above all, a chance to get out of bootcamp and East Prussia.

The Officers' Preparatory program actually turned out to be a lot of fun. It was an intensive six-week training period that would have been familiar to any of the thousands of "ninety-day wonders" pushed through the U.S. Army during the war. There were about four hundred prospective officer candidates at Heidelberg, and we were divided into classroom-sized groups for the duration of the course. We received lectures on every facet of war, strategy, and military intelligence. When we weren't listening to lectures, we were being tested on the material we learned the day before. It was a demanding schedule, but it made me realize how much I missed school and the process of education. Much of the information was routine, but one particular series of lectures turned out to have a significant influence on my life.

We were given instructions on how to elude the enemy in case we found ourselves trapped behind enemy lines. What fun! I was already intrigued by the subject, a curiosity triggered by the appearance of so many strangers in Schweidnitz and fueled by pulp novels and spy warnings in the government newspapers. I listened intently to every point in the lectures (never imagining, of course, that I would actually need such information), and I was thrilled to face the final test. All four hundred candidates were to pretend that we were escaped prisoners and that we had to elude capture in a hostile country. We were all taken to the outskirts of Heidelberg and instructed to make it to a point on the other side of town without being caught by our instructors. We would be graded on our ingenuity and ultimate success. I was so eager to try my skill that I could hardly sleep the night before the test.

Early the next morning, all four hundred of us were turned loose and the game was on! Some climbed over the rooftops, and other slogged through the sewer system. Some even posed as women to get past the checkpoints. Nevertheless they were caught in droves. In fact, every single one of them was caught—except me! My logic was simple, and so was the plan. My pursuers would expect the unusual, something cunning. Thus, I would do the obvious; the most normal thing, something they wouldn't expect. I got on a streetcar and rode across town. I presented myself to the startled instructors at the finish point before they had even had a chance to settle in. As a result, I graduated from the Officers' Preparatory School in the top five of the class (me!). My new official designation, listed on all military records after my name, was the coveted title: *Kriegsoffizierbewerber* (K.O.B.)—War Officer Candidate. Things were finally beginning to go my way; I could already see my officers' epaulets in the distance. Now I considered what I needed to do for that final but substantial leap to a commission. There was only one way: I had to get some frontline experience. Not too much experience, mind you; just enough to "get my ticket punched," as they say in the military. I thrilled at the thought of a new adventure, and the prospect of real combat brought my vision of Captain Horst Trispel back into focus. But if I didn't find a combat assignment on my own, and quickly, the army would decide for me—and considering my skiing experience, it might well be on the Russian front.

On the very day I graduated, in mid-April 1942, I saw an announcement on the school bulletin board. It was a call for volunteers for the Afrika Korps! Field Marshal Erwin Rommel's legendary Afrika Korps! The Desert Fox! Warm weather! That was for me! Adventure, combat experience, and travel; and all that in the warm desert sunshine. I sent in my application, and to my great astonishment, I was accepted! On May 1, 1942, I boarded a trooptrain crowded with other replacement soldiers bound for the coast of North Africa.

The trip itself was a series of grand adventures. After days on the train, we halted in Rome to await new transportation, and we were given sixty days' leave! How wonderful. My chums and I traveled all over Italy: Pompeii, Naples, all over. I even saw the pope. The next leg of our journey (by cattle train, this time) took us down through Yugoslavia to Greece, where, to our great delight, we were given another thirty days' leave. I thought this was terrific (though I could have done without the cattle train). This is why I joined the army! My friends and I toured Greece; we swam in the Adriatic and had our pictures taken with pretty girls. Horst Trispel, eat your heart out! From Athens we went by ship to Crete, and from there by air transport (on an old JU-52 trimotor, the workhorse of the German military) to North Africa. I arrived in January 1943, just in time to join Rommel's historic retreat before the overwhelming weight of British and American forces. The front-line experience necessary to enter Officers' School in Berlin was finally here.

THE AFRIKA KORPS was a unique experience. It was, of course, my baptism of fire, my first time in combat. Every man, I think, wonders how he would react in war. Would I be valiant? Heroic? A born leader? A victor? Or, as is every man's secret terror, will I break and run? Be a coward? Let my comrades down? Those questions bothered me more than any others as our JU-52 approached the coast of North Africa from Crete. To my great relief, I acquitted myself honorably and, on rare occasions, perhaps even bravely.

The second thing that made the experience unique was North Africa itself. It was another world! Due to my limited acquaintance of the world outside of Schweidnitz, I was even more astounded by my unbelievable new surroundings. The sights, the sounds. Every street I turned held new fascinations, and every merchant who hawked something (*"shufty, shufty"*—"look, look") introduced me to an intriguing item. I was enthralled by their elaborate (but often hypocritical) courtesies and by the brazenness of their bargaining. Even their name for us: "Teds" (from the Italian word for Germans, *Tedesco*), seemed interesting. Arab music was intriguing, as was their uncanny ability to materialize at every outpost, however far from civilization, to sell us trinkets and provide a one-day laundry service. It was from one of these Arabs that I bought my silver ring with the running antelope, one of the few personal items I took with me when I escaped from Camp Deming.

The weather was as unique to me as everything else in North Africa. I had grown up with normal seasons, most of them cold. Here I was in weather that plummeted from a hundred-something during the day, to below zero at night. Windstorms, called *"hamsins,"* periodically blew in for days, bringing the armies to a halt and making our lives unbearable with ever-present grit and sand. Ironically we often welcomed the wind as a respite to the clouds of flies, gnats, and mosquitoes that surrounded us. Still, it was beautiful; hostile and unforgiving of mistakes, but breathtakingly beautiful.

The last, and perhaps most exciting part of my service in North Africa was the élan of the Afrika Korps itself. What German schoolchild didn't follow the brilliant exploits of the *Panzerarmee Afrika* or know the words to the popular song *Panzer rollen in Afrika vor*? Rommel himself, of course, was almost worshiped in Germany. His photograph was on the cover of almost every magazine, and his book *Infantry Attacks* was mandatory reading for all budding military men. Rommel was a legend.

From 1939 to 1942 he had risen from colonel, commanding an obscure infantry school at Weiner Neustadt in the Austrian Alps, to field marshal, the highest rank in the German Army. He had commanded the Fuehrer's bodyguard in Poland, the 7th Panzer Division in France, and then the elite Afrika Korps, Panzer Army Afrika, and finally the entire Army Group Afrika in Libya, Egypt, and Tunisia. Time after time he had smashed numerically superior armies at places like Sidi Rezegh, Sollum, Gazala, Benghazi, Tobruk, and the Kasserine Pass. He was finally beaten at El Alamein by the equally respected Field Marshal Bernard Montgomery in a battle fought with extraordinary skill and valor by both sides. On November 4, 1942, after a harrowing battle that was fought along a line extending thirty-eight miles from the sea southward into the Libyan desert, Rommel's dazzlingly successful drive eastward to Cairo was stopped dead. The battle of El Alamein cost Rommel 55,000 men out of the 108,000 with which he started and reduced the surviving German and Italian divisions to shambles.

Lost were most of the Mark III and Mark IV Panzer tanks that had previously ruled the desert war with their short, low-velocity 75mm guns and redesigned long-barreled 50mm artillery pieces. Lost also were many of the famous 88mm antiaircraft guns that had so successfully decimated Montgomery's Matilda and Crusader tanks in the past. The route had begun. In the words of Winston Churchill: "Before Alamein we never had a victory; after Alamein, we never had a defeat." Rommel knew that North Africa was lost, but Hitler wouldn't hear of it. Thus began the westward retreat of what remained of the vaunted Afrika Korps and the remnants of the Italian army; slowly at first, with as much equipment as possible, then helter-skelter, abandoning everything that became a hindrance to the dash for survival. Our retreating army was now forced to rely on ferocious rearguard actions and diabolical mines and boobytraps. The balance of military power in North Africa was clearly in Allied hands, and their ranks swelled with new weapons and fresh troops. For the next four months, from January to April 1943, *Panzerarmee Afrika* was hounded for 1,500 miles to the final showdown at the city of Tunis, in the westernmost corner of North Africa. Rommel badly needed replacement troops, and a call for volunteers was trumpeted across Germany. Such a call appeared on the bulletin board of the Officers' Preparatory School in Heidelberg on the very day I graduated from training, and I arrived in North Africa in time to join the final retreat toward Tunisia and surrender.

Of course, I had no idea about the military realities of the war as our plane approached German-occupied Tripoli. We had long grown used to disregarding any government version of anything, especially news from the front lines. The government hád "managed the news" for so many years that no one but the most convinced Nazis believed anything we read in the newspapers. We were continuously told that our factories were producing record numbers of everything, that our harvests were more bountiful than ever before, and that other nations were always conspiring against us. Somehow, thanks to the Nazi Party, we were always winning or overproducing, and only the slackards and internal dissidents among us prevented Germany from achieving the "Final Victory" (whatever that was). Military news was even less believable: our forces were always heroic, we sustained few casualties, and the enemy was always cunning in battle and craven in defeat. We simply looked at the dramatic headlines and shrugged.

Then came the attack on Russia on June 22, 1941. Even the most pro-Nazi Germans were apprehensive about the logic of such an awesome invasion—a fear underscored by the horror stories brought back by soldiers home on leave from the Eastern Front. Every indicator told us that we were losing terribly—the growing casualty lists, the patriotic campaigns to collect warm clothing for the troops (why hadn't the army prepared for such a basic problem?), and then the whispered accounts of savage fighting, mass deaths, and military reversals. Berlin countered our growing despondency by sending soldiers on leave to distant rest areas where they could not enlighten friends and families, by censoring all mail from the front lines, and giving us dramatic headlines of impending victory. On at least nine separate occasions (to my personal knowledge) the official party newspaper, the *Völkischer Beobachter (The People's Observer),* declared our triumphant march into Moscow and the final Russian surrender. Little wonder, then, that we paid little serious attention to any official communiques. Thus, as our lumbering trimotor cargo plane brought us into Tripoli on January 20, 1943, I had no idea that I was about to join the desperate rout of the German Army in North Africa. I had a strong feeling that we were in serious trouble but hoped for the best.

Whatever doubts I had were soon confirmed as we were unceremoniously ordered out of the plane to stand blinking and bewildered in the stifling Libyan sun as senior officers and classified military files were loaded for rapid departure. Within the hour, the airfield came under an artillery bombardment by what we soon learned was Montgomery's Eighth Army, our nemesis for the remainder of the campaign. My first hour in North Africa, and I was huddled in a shell hole while shouting men rushed to save the storehouses of ammunition and drums of precious fuel. So much for my newly issued khaki desert uniform with the silver stripe of an officer's candidate on my shoulder epaulets. Dirt and sand showered over me, and the suffocating heat was punctuated by the whining sounds of hot steel splinters as I tried to assess my new situation. Heroism was for the birds, I quickly concluded, and the best thing to do for myself and my country would be to survive intact. Never mind the romance of war and the camaraderie of men singing the haunting refrain of "Lilli Marlene" in the late evening safety of their foxholes. After two hours of combat, I had had all the experience I cared for. When the smoke and noise had cleared, I ventured out of my burrow and faced the future. I was assigned to my new unit, the Panzer Artillery Regiment 33rd of the legendary 15th Panzer Division and joined the tens of thousands of German and Italian troops retreating westward toward the corner of Tunisia. Behind us was the relentless British Eighth Army. Tripoli, and the airport where I had arrived, fell to Montgomery three days later on January 23.

The next three months were hellish. I can't think of a better word. My unit was composed of twelve huge 105mm guns; real monsters pulled by half-tracks that fired a thirty-pound projectile of high explosive six to ten miles. Awesome weapons. The shells were nearly three feet high and the noise deafening enough to cause me to have diminished hearing in both ears to this day. Each gun had a crew of six men who loaded the shells, drove the half-tracks, and kept the breaches cleaned and oiled. Then there were the assorted ordnance mechanics and men responsible for hauling and distributing the cases of ammunition. Lastly, and with some sarcasm in my list of priorities, came several officers—tough veterans of earlier battles whose aloofness from their men made them seem remote and almost superfluous—whose task was to direct our fire based on map coordinates radioed to them from the front lines. We would hear the explosions of battle miles away, for example, and await our coordinates. A front-line officer would radio the information to us, and we would be galvanized into action. First, we lobbed a shell just to see where we were aimed (and heaven help our own troops if we were firing "short"). Then we were instructed from the front (sometimes the rear) as to how many degrees we should readjust the gun: ten degrees up or down, so many degrees to the left

50

or right, until we were "on target." That's what we did. And, as the new sergeant, I was assigned the noisiest job: after confirming each new set of coordinates and supervising the loading of the fifty-pound shell, I pulled the lanyard that caused the earth to shudder and to leave my ears ringing for thirty minutes. I often shouted a derogatory remark about Horst Trispel as I snapped the lanyard and braced for the concussion. Come to think of it, my unheard curses included our officers, their officers—Rommel and Montgomery, Hitler and Eisenhower. My shouts didn't change anything, of course, but I felt better.

The real danger in our jobs lay in the enemy's determined efforts to knock us out of action. Often the British would bring up their big guns, and the terrifying artillery duel would begin. Our spotters would strain through binoculars to see our explosions and frantically call out new coordinates in the hope that we would knock out the enemy guns before the explosions advancing toward us, directed by their spotters, could find us. Their gunners were every bit as capable as ours, and victory hinged on each crew's ability to correct, load, and fire before the enemy did. Our lives depended on teamwork and blind luck.

Even more dangerous than the artillery duels were the planes. Nothing in my life has been as frightening or as harrowing as the sudden appearance of a string of American P-38 or P-40 fighter planes, guns blazing, as they descended on us out of the afternoon sun. A shout of *"Flugzeug!"* and we would scramble off the guns and dive into shallow foxholes even as the first bullets began to whine around us. The planes usually made half-a-dozen strafing runs, their guns stitching through our ranks, before they either ran out of ammunition or moved on to a better target. I cannot imagine a more vulnerable feeling than being curled up in a shallow hole (grave?), completely visible, as planes shriek out of the sky—often at treetop level (had there been trees)—to seek you out and kill you. Our only safety lay in spreading our foxholes over a large distance, what Rommel called "removing the bulls-eyes from the targets." We were often dug-in hundreds of yards apart, and while it was terribly lonely, at least we made an unattractive target for low-flying enemy planes. I still have occasional nightmares about those planes. I quickly learned that nothing was more important than having that foxhole, and since our unit moved almost daily, turning back only to delay the relentless advance of Montgomery's army, I must have hacked out a hundred foxholes in the hard, rocky ground of North Africa.

That, then, was the general pattern of my days and weeks (and months) in the Afrika Korps. We were fighting a massive delaying action: artillery duels over a front thirty or forty miles wide; then we'd quickly haul the guns a few miles westward, turn and bombard the enemy again. Sometimes our rear-guard troops would hold the enemy to a standstill for several days, and we would settle into our little pits to read an old tattered issue of the Korps newspaper, *Die Oase (The Oasis)*, or write letters home, or simply sleep. However welcome, a peaceful afternoon also meant hours in the blinding sunlight, blankets of savage flies, and a pall of emotional depression as we had a quiet opportunity to contemplate our minor role in a losing battle and the decreasing chances that we would come out of this unharmed. The routine was only broken by the arrival of a paymaster who paid us once in Deutschmarks, the next time in Italian lira, and from then on in cigarettes and soap that we could trade to the ever-present Arabs who materialized during any lull in the fighting. Although we readily agreed that the money would not do us much good out in the desert, we viewed the change in currencies as a bad sign. Which, of course, it was.

We were retreating forty to fifty miles a day, as more than a hundred thousand German and Italian troops, many now racked by disease and dysentery, rushed to round the western corner of North Africa and escape southward. The British were gobbling up the terrain behind us, and we heard frequent rumors about our former positions engulfed by the enemy only days after we departed. We grew used to seeing burned-out tanks along the sides of the roads, the broken bodies of their crews draped on the wrecks. We were in real trouble and we knew it. The coastal city of Medenine fell to the British on February 17, 1943, as we rolled into the Tunisian desert. We tried to turn southward but found that we had been outflanked by American forces at Gafsa, Tebessa, the Kasserine Pass, and Sbiba. While Rommel continued to acquit himself brilliantly, it was clear that the *Panzerarmee Afrika* was being boxed into the Tunisian pocket. Rommel tried a desperate breakout on March 9, turning back on the British at Medenine with the full force of all three of our Panzer divisions, the 10th, 15th, and 21st. We were repulsed, losing one-third of our armored strength. It was the beginning of the end. Unbeknownst to us common soldiers, Rommel was ordered home in semidisgrace in March, and Army Group Afrika was taken over by Colonel General Jurgen von Arnim, a veteran of the Russian front. Nine weeks later the Fifth Panzer Army, the First German-Italian Army, and the elite Afrika Korps were destroyed. Von Arnim was forced to surrender to the Allies (he was sent to a special VIP camp for high-ranking German officers at Clinton, Mississippi), and for 130,000 German and Italian soldiers (Georg Gaertner among them) the war was over.

We knew nothing about such grand plans, of course. Like ground soldiers the world over, I was only aware of the events that occurred in the thirty-yard radius around my foxhole. For me, the grand plan was simply to go where I was ordered and try to survive the flies and the heat, the strafing planes and artillery duels, and the privations that go with a mass retreat on behalf of a lost cause. March progressed to April, and we knew that the end could not be far off. Our army was now boxed into the Tunisian peninsula, and we were being herded toward the coastal cities of Tunis and Bizerte. Now I received orders to go to Berlin to complete my officers' training course and receive my commission. But I couldn't leave. We were surrounded! Abruptly, one day in mid-April 1943, everything stopped. It was the eeriest thing: it suddenly became very still. No planes, no artillery fire in the distance, no whistles or commands—just silence. We just sat in our far-flung line of foxholes and awaited orders. By evening our officers were going from foxhole to foxhole telling us to relax and await further orders. The next day we were told that we were now out of the fighting and that British soldiers would be by to pick us up in trucks in the next few days. Curiously, after months of terrible fighting, I suddenly felt no bitterness toward the enemy. Both sides had fought well, and they had just won, that's all. I was drained of any emotion. Worn out. And relieved that it was finally over.

We stretched out in our little foxholes for three solid days, reading tattered novels distributed by a passing German Red Cross representative, hooting calls from foxhole to foxhole, and dozing in the late afternoon sunshine. Suddenly we saw soldiers in British desert shorts fanning out toward us, within moments they were gently helping us to our feet and into line. We saw that the winners were worn out too. We threw away our cumbersome regulation helmets in favor of the comfortable long-billed caps of the Afrika Korps and rose unsteadily to become prisoners of war.

I went through the next few weeks in a daze. Most of us were too tired to talk. We went where we were told and numbly answered the many routine questions asked. Army personnel were separated from air force and officers from enlisted men. We were registered, fingerprinted, photographed, and our names forwarded to the Swiss and the International Red

Cross Committee for relay to our worried families. My new identity was POW #81 [designation for captives of the North African campaign] G [German] 80392. We were searched for weapons and military papers, but not being officers we had neither. That fact never seemed to bother our captors who viewed us as a continual source of war souvenirs. At each stage of our shipment to the huge Allied holding pens at Oran we were searched repeatedly for any piece of Nazi equipment—medals, decorations, daggers, or Lugers—that might have escaped the notice of the previous searchers. Then, like small tributaries of a stream, we joined larger rivers of fellow captives, and we trudged and rode toward Oran.

After several days we were turned over to the Americans who guarded us the rest of the way. What interesting people, those Americans. What struck me first was their robust health. Everyone looked overweight and for a short time I even wondered if their weight was the reason they all rode in jeeps. Clearly they had only recently arrived in North Africa and did not yet have the "dietary benefit" of several months on army rations in desert combat. My next surprise was seeing black people. We did not have Negroes in Germany and as odd as it may seem today, I simply had never seen black people. A handsome-looking black sergeant even spoke to me in perfect German! I was too startled to answer, so he just shrugged, muttered something about my being a "Dummkopf" and walked on. I was also struck by the astonishing amount of equipment they had: every imaginable type of vehicle and weapon. Yet, it was a small nagging detail that suddenly made me realize that I was looking at more than well-equipped American guards. I was looking at the victors of the war. It was the nonchalance with which they let their engines idle without any concern for a shortage of fuel. At that moment I realized that we would lose the war. Germany was foolish enough to have declared war on a country whose resources seemed almost limitless. America would simply overproduce us to defeat. Lastly, I was impressed by their informality. Saluting was minimal, and their conversations with one another (and us) were generally open and friendly. I liked Americans from the very beginning although they had several traits that would take some getting used to: their need to approach life on a first-name basis; a disinterest in learning about art and history, their own no less than anyone else's; and an unshakeable belief that any problem could be overcome by devising a bigger or costlier solution. Flaws or not, I liked them from the first moment. They represented something I had never had before: freedom. And how I yearned for freedom!

The next step was the trip to the United States. From collection areas across North Africa, all newly registered prisoners were funneled by the truckloads to "reception centers" at Casablanca, Morocco, and Oran, Algeria. My "reception center" at Oran contained nearly ten thousand (!) German and Italian prisoners of war in an enormous barbed wire enclosure. Imagine ten thousand men milling about from morning to night: chatting, sullen, seeking out lost comrades, bartering cigarettes, exchanging rumors, and staking out a spot to sleep. We received books and writing paper from the American, International, and German Red Cross, and spent our time doing what soldiers seemed to be trained for: waiting. During the several weeks I spent in the holding center, June 1943, I slowly developed the habits and hobbies that sustained me for the next two years of imprisonment in the United States. I learned to create little things out of available wood or leather: cigarette cases, belts, wallets, carved items. I became a loner, relying only on myself. One never knew the politics or the motives of the people around you, a lesson already ingrained since childhood in Nazi Germany. I tried not to form deep friendships with any of the other POWs since we would probably be sent to different camps or separated by an unforeseen military routine. Oh, I always had lots of chums, friends with whom I could spend an evening playing cards in the camp canteen or discussing art during a leisurely walk across the camp grounds. But no strong bonds. Not only was it the logical way to prepare for an ocean voyage to a strange country, and the years in confinement ahead, but it fit well with my personality. I had long been a loner and chafed at any restrictions in my life. In retrospect, it is astonishing how my personality, outlook, and skills were preparing me for nearly forty years as a fugitive.

One day at the end of June, an empty Liberty ship became available and the embarkation process shifted into high gear so we could clear the area and link up with other ships forming convoys across the Atlantic. What excitement! The twenty-three-year-old kid from rural Schweidnitz was crossing the ocean to the United States! Even Horst couldn't beat this. The ship was cramped, with POWs sleeping three bunks high. Most of our time was spent in our bunks, although on occasion we were allowed topside to enjoy the fresh ocean breeze or catch a smoke. On one of those trips to the deck, an American MP noticed my handmade cigarette case and offered me a dollar for it. After a thoughtful pause I learned from the Arab hawkers, I gave in. That small event, which still warms me to this day, had a curious effect on my life. It fanned the ember of a budding artistic talent that had only found an outlet through architecture (I have since held one-man gallery shows and regularly sell my paintings for substantial sums of money). The sale of that silly cigarette case to the young MP had another important effect: it cemented my affection for Americans. The exchange of something I had created, in return for something equally dear to a young American enlisted man (the dollar), made me feel—even at that moment—that I had made a bond with my future. I was going to be an American.

The trip was otherwise uneventful. Strict discipline was maintained by German officers, as always, and they, in turn, dutifully saluted all Americans of senior rank. (I'll never understand the military mind: one minute we were killing each other, and the next we were offering the most courteous military respect.) The most difficult problems with which we POWs had to contend during the voyage were frequent seasickness and inadequate exercise and ventilation, conditions familiar to any American soldier transported overseas. Otherwise, our routine was only broken by occasional delousing programs, filling out forms for the Swiss or Red Cross, and those damned searches for war souvenirs. (It was becoming clear that the further we were from the front lines, the more determined the souvenir hunters who realized that we prisoners were as close as they would probably get to the war. I mean, they were already taking our uniform buttons!) I count myself lucky that I still had most of my Afrika Korps uniform when the ship docked in New York in mid-August. Again we were processed, deloused, and, of course, searched. Then we were marched onto waiting trains.

The train ride to my first POW camp at McLean, Texas (by the end of the war I would be routinely shifted to four more camps), was perhaps the most impressive ten days of my young life. Under the watchful gaze of the two armed MPs strolling up and down the aisle of our coach car, we sat with our faces pressed to the windows. America was endless, it seemed to us, and we sat entranced as it passed before us. Bustling cities, tiny hamlets, forests and flatland, and, my God, the number of cars! We simply didn't realize how big America was, a fact that now convinced most of us that escape was futile. While a few die-hard Nazis continued to mutter that we were obviously being routed away from the bomb-damaged cities, or that we were fortunate to be in America as a welcoming force for Hitler's eventual invasion, the majority of us settled in, humbled and homesick, as we watched the landscape change to the vast treeless prairie of north-central Texas and POW Camp McLean.

THERE WERE MORE than one hundred fifty POW base camps across the country, each with about two thousand to four thousand men, and literally hundreds of small satellite camps of perhaps two hundred to three hundred men constructed to bring us closer to the harvests or work sites. Each base camp, like McLean, was built according to a standard layout by the Corps of Engineers. The camp was divided into four compounds of approximately five hundred to seven hundred fifty men each, and each compound, in turn, consisted of four barracks with about one hundred fifty men. Walkways and gravel roads ran throughout the camp. Most base camps had a wide assortment of administrative buildings, mess halls, infirmaries, canteens, workshops, and warehouses, as well as a post office, chapel, showers, and laundry. In fact, the only real differences between our POW camps and normal army training centers were the watchtowers, the two wire fences, ten-feet high and eight-feet apart, the searchlights and occasional dog patrols.

Actually, I liked Camp McLean. It was brand-new and sparkling clean. We felt like pioneer settlers, in a way; out on the prairie and miles from civilization. Moving in was kind of exciting: putting up favorite pictures or pin-ups torn from American magazines, and making one's little area livable. It was as close to having a real home as any of us had had since we left Germany, and I was pretty comfortable there. The food was terrific: meat, vegetables, milk, desserts, even wine and beer on occasion at the camp canteen. There were plenty of handicraft and educational programs to keep us occupied, though no grown man could completely escape the boredom of confinement. Red Cross officials and local churchmen regularly checked on our needs for sports equipment, musical instruments, and reading material. The weather was gorgeous, and our only military responsibility was to line up every morning in the bright clear sunshine to be counted and salute the American officer in charge. Since I spoke English reasonably well, I was called upon to translate orders and directives from the camp authorities, and forward prisoner requisitions, petitions, and occasional protests.

In a very deep sense, the eight months I spent at McLean, Texas, altered my life. I fell in love with the West. Vast, silent, rugged, and beautiful. Like most Europeans I had grown up reading Karl May westerns: Aryan cowboys locked in mortal combat with savage (though sometimes noble) Red Men. (Hitler's radio broadcasts often mentioned some heroic struggle in a Karl May novel to illustrate a new demand for Germany's continued sacrifice. I firmly believe that Hitler declared war on an America created from the wildly inaccurate picture painted by Karl May.) Yet, however industrial and populated the East Coast, the West was really as I had imagined it when Horst, Heinz, Ursula, Susan, and I crept stealthily through the parks of Schweidnitz in search of wily Indians. In a way, my escape from Camp Deming, New Mexico, two years later, was as much an embrace of the American West as it was a fear of returning to Soviet Germany. The West represents the purest form of freedom and self-reliance, independence, and kinship with nature. In fact, during the four decades since my escape I have rarely left the West Coast. While the FBI was scouring the urban centers of New York and Chicago, and Army Intelligence units were interviewing my old classmates from Oberreal Schule for clues to my hiding place in the French Zone of Germany (?), I was living and working in places like San Pedro, Santa Cruz, Palo Alto, and San Francisco. My love of the West Coast and its folklore has never diminished.

I was in Camp McLean from August 28, 1943, until April 27, 1944, and was sad when several of us received orders to be transferred to Camp Mexia (pronounced Ma-hay-ya). Such transfers occurred routinely for reasons we could never fathom, but I was nonetheless sorry to leave. Camp Mexia turned out to be equally nice, and I developed a deep fondness for the green expanses of East Texas. The camp layout was about the same, as was my job, though I branched out to work as a camp draftsman. Otherwise, it was the same routine as at McLean. I was a POW at Mexia from May 16, 1944, until December 28, when yet another shipment order came through. This time it was to the POW compound attached to Fort Knox, Kentucky. I had hardly settled in—I was there only fifteen days— when a group of us were transferred once again. (In the military, one learns to accept crackpot decisions with a sense of bewildered tolerance.) To my delight, my new home was Camp Huntsville in the hill country of central Texas. As before, the layout and routine were generally the same as at the earlier camps. I enjoyed Camp Huntsville and was saddened but hardly surprised when, six months later, on June 5, 1945, a bunch of us were told to pack our belongings once again. Now it was Camp Lordsburg, New Mexico, though not for long. I probably saw more of the western United States in two years than most Americans do in a lifetime. After a few days at Lordsburg, I was told that my presence was now wanted at the branch camp at Deming, fifty-six miles east.

As much as I loved adventure, I was getting pretty tired of packing and unpacking, of never knowing whether I could risk getting comfortable or begin making friends. As the truck from Lordsburg brought us through the main gate at Camp Deming and we stared vacantly at the military ritual of signing us over to the new camp officials, I silently vowed that this would be my last camp of the war. In fact, the European war was over the month before, and I was reaching the saturation point regarding the military — ours and theirs. I was sick of taking orders and responding to mindless routine. Yes, I promised myself, this would be my last camp in America.

Not only was I about finished with military life, but conditions in the POW camps were deteriorating quickly. Now that America's liberated prisoners were returning from overseas, the quality of our food dropped sharply and general treatment hardened. Revelations about the Nazi atrocities were making our guards dangerously edgy, and we watched our fate angrily debated in the newspapers. Clearly, it was time for this epoch to end. We weighed all the options available to the War Department and generally assumed that we would ultimately be discharged in the American Zone of West Germany. We also agreed that it might not be the ideal place to end up, considering the widespread hunger and postwar chaos, but it was a damn sight better than ending up in Russian hands. God, just don't let me be turned over to the Russians . . . the Russians . . . the Russians . . .

SUDDENLY MY BODY was jolted forward, and I realized that I was huddled in the dark corner of a boxcar lurching to a stop. All at once I was starving, cold, and terrified. What had I done? Before I could even take stock of my situation I realized that the train was stopping. We had reached our destination. Survival now depended on getting out of the boxcar before I was discovered by the approaching railroad detectives who were peering into each car. My heart was pounding as I lowered myself quietly out of the boxcar. I shrank back as I waited for the men to turn away. For a brief moment all three appeared to be distracted by something at the front of the train and I bolted away from the car. I scrambled up a gravel embankment and ran as far as my weakened condition allowed. After a few hundred yards my legs gave out, and I crouched in the shadows of a railroad warehouse. I hadn't been spotted. I gathered my courage and remaining strength and walked out of the railroad yard unchallenged. So far, so good. But where in the hell was I? As I stood blinking in the bright sunlight, trying to collect my thoughts, I saw a large sign painted across one of the railroad yard buildings. It read: SAN PEDRO, CALIFORNIA. I can still recall that soaring moment and the joy I felt. I had made it!!

THREE

CALIFORNIA! HOW FITTING that the only train passing my POW camp at Deming would have been destined for California. America's last frontier. Larger than many European countries, California comprised nearly a thousand miles of breathtaking coastline, year 'round sunshine, and an almost defiant sense of rugged individualism. It was the place for me!

For almost two hundred years, American pioneers had moved westward, prospectors and ranchers, businessmen and holy men, dreamers and schemers. When they reached the shores of the vast Pacific Ocean they were in California, and most of them stayed. Their descendants, I found, represented the widest diversity of social, economic, and political elements in America, and, with some shameful exceptions, California tolerated them all. It was the place to experiment, to build something new. In the words of John Steinbeck, California was less a state of the union than a state of mind. In more realistic terms, California was a mecca for three basic types of people: farsighted entrepreneurs in search of riches; the disinherited poor looking for jobs and cheap housing; and finally, a broad spectrum of adventurous pleasure-seekers who benefited from the luxuries of the rich and exploited the labor of the poor. It was both the end of the rainbow and the end of the line.

Looking back, I still marvel at the blind luck which brought me to California. Here I was: a terrified youngster of twenty-five, only days removed from the German Army; an escaped fugitive speaking broken

English in a strange country. I had no idea about the customs and laws of the people around me. In fact, my only knowledge about Americans up to that point was through infrequent exchanges with our POW guards, reading American newspapers, and the old-fashioned, stilted vocabulary of Karl May's novels ("Lo, the desperados approach us with haste!"). In retrospect, I seriously doubt if I could have survived as easily anywhere but in California. Where would I have found a warm place to live in Chicago, for instance, or New York? How would I eat until I found work? Here I could sleep outdoors under a balmy sky and pluck fruit where I found it. In places like Ames, Iowa, or Litchfield, Connecticut, not to mention states with a southern drawl like Georgia, Mississippi, or Alabama, I would have stuck out like a sore thumb. What if I had ended up in a predominantly ethnic or religious community where my appearance would have aroused immediate curiosity? No, I doubt if I could have remained at large for more than a week anywhere but California. Moreover, with the end of the war, new residents were arriving by the thousands in search of employment, wealth, or a new start. I simply became one of them.

How fortunate that my new start would begin in San Pedro. The famous Port of Los Angeles, gateway to the Pacific, is in reality the basin coastline of several communities, thirty miles from the inland metropolis of Los Angeles. At the southern point of the harbor is Long Beach, and at the northern point, on a major cape, is the city of San Pedro. It was an easy city in which to disappear. A burly shipping and rail community of nearly 50,000 people, San Pedro boasted a large harbor district, a large military base at Fort MacArthur, and miles of distant Union Oil derricks and storage tanks. Culturally, one could enjoy the serenity of the Buddhist temple in East San Pedro, the opulent Royal Palms Country Club at White Point cove, or gaudy Beacon Street teeming with soldiers and sailors on Saturday night. For the younger set, San Pedro also had one of the first drive-in restaurants (The Harbor Drive-In on the corner of Sixth and Gaffey) in Southern California. It was a perfect city for me to begin the final leg of my escape. It was logically laid out, which meant that I would not get lost often or need to ask directions; it had enclaves of Yugoslavs and Italians, so I wouldn't stand out; large open areas to sleep—White Point Park, Royal Palms State Park, MacArthur Park, and Cabrillo Beach; and miles of docks and wharfs at the mouth of the Los Angeles Channel and along the adjacent Terminal Island. I was as good as gone.

But where did I want to go? I quickly decided that Europe was out.

Postwar Germany was in shambles: bombed-out cities, starvation conditions, ration books, identification cards, and questionnaires to ferret out the most dangerous Nazis for trial. None of that sounded remotely attractive to me. Besides, where would I go in Germany that was safer than here in the United States? Schweidnitz was now under the Soviets, and my poor parents most likely already dead or in a Russian labor camp. Moreover, the need for new identification papers almost assured that I would soon be arrested as an escaped POW and punished. No, Europe was out.

Then I thought about smuggling myself aboard a freighter bound for South America. Many Latin American countries were pro-German; some, like Argentina and Paraguay, were almost openly Nazi. I was sure that as a former Afrika Korps veteran I would be welcomed by the authorities and easily integrated into the culture. But the longer I reflected the more distasteful I found such a new life. Why would I want to live in a country that admired and emulated the very fascism I had grown to hate? Besides, I was enthralled with America and spoke some English. In any case, I had no idea which of the many huge ships being loaded and unloaded along the wharfs were bound for Europe, South America, or, for that matter, Alaska or Zanzibar. For weeks I slept in the city parks and spent my days prowling the heavily patrolled docks in search of a "sign." Perhaps I would overhear a stevedore shout a ship's destination, or stumble across an unguarded ramp. I soon realized that no "sign" was apparently forthcoming, and that my daily furtive skulking around the docks was sure to attract suspicion. In mid-October, four weeks after I had escaped from Camp Deming, I decided to temporarily abandon my plan to sneak aboard a foreign ship and instead try to make the best of the situation in America. I could always try another port if things didn't work out. With that decision I subconsciously committed myself to life in the United States. I decided to give it my best shot and for however long it might last, become the best damn American this country had ever seen.

I was terrified. It's difficult for anyone who has led a stable and secure life to imagine the constant fear of a fugitive, and a foreigner on top of it. Terror and anxiety permeate every moment, every pore, every thought. The most harmless stare or hint of passing interest causes instant panic. Do they know? Have I slipped up? Is someone pointing me out or even calling the police at this moment? I was frightened every waking moment. What happens if I'm stopped by a local policeman? I have to have a cover story ready at all times. For a while I practiced being a Yugoslavian refugee recently arrived from a Displaced Persons camp in Europe. What date did I arrive? What was the name of my ship? Who did I know in the Yugoslav community of San Pedro? Then I considered being French Canadian, then Dutch, then Latvian or Estonian (who knew anything about Latvians or Estonians?). I even considered being a deaf-mute, perhaps the result of some war wound. The dilemma solved itself one afternoon when I took my courage in hand and entered a small side-street barber shop. My hair was getting shaggy, and I was beginning to stand out among the crew cuts of the returning soldiers and other men my age. Sitting in the chair, my heart pounding at the possibility of saying something that might draw undue attention, I understood the barber to ask me if I was Norwegian. He said I resembled his brother-in-law in Michigan, a nice Norwegian lumberjack named Peter Peterson. I congratulated him on his keen eye. When I walked back out on to the street, I had a new identity: I was a Norwegian immigrant named Peter Peterson. Pretty unimaginative, I know, but it seemed reasonable at the time. I figured that if a San Pedro barber thought I was Norwegian, a man who prided himself on his ability to "size up" his customers, then that's what I would be. When I finally decided to move in out of the parks and risked renting a 50-cent-a-night room in a local boarding house, I signed the register as "Peter Peterson." I even bought a large silver belt buckle at an Army-Navy store on Beacon Street and had my new name engraved across it (in case I needed to substantiate my identity or, for that matter, remember my unfamiliar new name in the middle of the night). I remained "Peter Peterson" for more than a year.

Finding work was another heart-pounder. I began by answering signs in restaurant windows looking for dishwashers or busboys. Such menial work required no conversation, identification, or job application. Dishwashers and busboys were generally paid daily in cash and, when no one was watching, usually ate as well as the paying customers in the dining room. It was the kind of job that one could quit after a week or two. The "Dishwasher Wanted" sign would go back in the window and another drifter would apply. I'll bet I changed dishwasher jobs fifteen times in three months; any excessive interest by the kitchen help or the restaurant manager and I'd excuse myself to use the washroom, walk out the side door and simply never return. If my pay was somehow delayed or I was unexpectedly asked to fill out a detailed application, I walked. I knew that with the number of people arriving daily in California, the restaurants and sandwich shops had no difficulty hiring a replacement. I also changed rooming houses regularly, sometimes abruptly enough to leave my meager belongings behind. I must have replaced my cheap cardboard suitcase five times.

But earning eating money and changing rooms were only minor concerns in comparison to my central obsession: I had to learn to be American. Changing my identity and abandoning my language, habits, and past was the most wrenching trauma of my life. Indeed, one could say that my entire adult life has been an ongoing perfection of my new identity. I literally had to become another person. No habit or viewpoint was too insignificant to be evaluated and, if necessary, purged. I had to change the way I walked, from my German (military) stride to an ambling gait; the way I shook hands (I had to stop snapping my head down and automatically shaking hands with women); even the tunes I might aimlessly whistle (Benny Goodman was in, *"Deutschland über Alles"* was out).

Americans simply cannot fathom the reeducation that thousands of immigrants around them have to undergo. I had to learn to part my hair, for example, instead of combing it straight back in the European fashion. I learned to eat my biggest meal in the evening rather than at noon as we did in the old country; and to approach life with an informality bordering on rudeness. Then there was the use of silverware! Europeans eat with the knife in one hand and the fork in the other (still the most logical way of eating if you ask me). It took me months to become comfortable with the curious habit of relying on the fork alone and changing hands to use the knife. And that was only the beginning. Every day I was startled and confused by new customs and phrases.

Hitting a "home run," I found, was doing something correctly; "striking out" was failing; and "getting to first base" generally meant an enjoyable evening with a young lady. I learned that "Count" Basie, Nat "King" Cole, and "Duke" Ellington were not royalty, and that music came in "longhair," "swing," "rag-time," and "be-bop." Think of the number of slang words for money alone: bucks, lettuce, smazzolas, moolah, greenbacks, sawbucks, five-spots, C-notes, two-bits, etc. Or the military jargon in our vocabulary, like AWOL, ASAP, SNAFU, and so forth. One could be "on the make," "on the take," "on the sauce," or "on the wagon." I found that words like "rough" and "tough" did not enable me to pronounce "dough," and that lofty speeches about democracy did not prepare me for drinking fountains and waiting rooms marked "White" and "Colored." I also learned that John could be Jack, James could be Jim, Robert could be Bob, and that I was invariably Pete.

Every day was a new and frightening adventure. What if I made a mistake? What if I said something without thinking? For years I had automatically lifted my hand in the (meaningless) Hitler greeting to German shopkeepers and passing strangers; what if I slipped in San Pedro, California? I had been in the military for almost five years; what if I inadvertently barked *"Jawohl!"* to a restaurant manager's orders? My Norwegian story could only cover so many errors before people would become suspicious. Of course, all new immigrants risk ridicule with each word and gesture, but in my case the penalty would be arrest, imprisonment, and deportation to Soviet-occupied Germany. Consequently, I had to be extremely cautious while I worked furiously to better my halting English and purge myself of every vestige of my German past. Moreover, I couldn't share my secret with anyone. Close friends and romances were out of the question. I had to adapt alone and fast. I never went to sleep at night, then or now, without examining the day's events in detail, looking for any slip-up in my behavior and bracing myself for the events of the following day.

It was also becoming clear that my excessive caution and frantic efforts to blend into my new country were motivated by more than the terror of arrest and deportation. I realized that I really wanted to stay in America and, perhaps, someday, even become a legal citizen. That soon became my secret fantasy. As a result, and unlike most hunted fugitives, I never consciously broke any law and I paid my taxes every year without fail (under whatever name I was then using). Like millions of immigrants who came to the United States before me, I was grateful to be here.

What a marvelous country, America. The abundance of food and goods, the acceptance of diverse opinions and life-styles, and the generosity of its people is truly unique. There isn't another country in the world, I assure you, that offers free matches in restaurants; free pencils, notepaper, and soap in hotels; free road maps in gas stations; free rolls and crackers at the lunch counter; free peanuts and pretzels at the bar; free samples in the mail—the abundance of America astonishes me to this day.

The mobility of Americans impressed me as well. Europeans seldom moved from one city to another, or, for that matter, from one apartment building to another. Generations of families were rooted to their communities, come fire, flood, or civil insurrection. Wars and famine may interrupt the continuity of life, but the survivors return to their homes. Europeans who do choose to relocate, however, face a blizzard of bureaucratic red tape and required permits. And the same applies to work. Europeans of my generation could not simply change jobs at will. Men and women were required to have a labor passbook that contained their complete work history, and a change of jobs meant signatures, certification of union dues paid, and comments on the quality of work performed. What a liberating feeling it was for me to change addresses or look for a new job whenever the mood struck me. And what a joy to live without an ever-present identification card. Here one didn't need to identify oneself at the whim of a petty bureaucrat, hotel manager, or factory supervisor. I think the best example of this unique independence is illustrated by an episode that happened to a friend of mine. He had been stopped by a policeman for failing to have his dog on a leash in a Denver park. The cop started to write him a ticket and asked his name. "John Jones," my friend Steven responded, irritated at the ponderousness with which the policeman treated the trivial issue. The cop demanded to see some identification that, my friend assured him, was not required by law. He said that he didn't drive a car and therefore didn't have a driver's license; he had been in the military so he no longer needed to carry a draft card; and he didn't read often enough to need a library card. Finally, the policeman threw up his hands and let him off with a stern warning. In Germany the inability to produce an official identification card, not to mention such defiance of authority, would have had serious consequences. But not in America.

To my great relief I was never required to produce an I.D. card during my early years in the United States. The war was over, and Americans were fed up with official forms, ration books, draft cards, V-Mail stationery, and the like. It was time to enjoy peace and victory. Moreover, the nation was on the move. Demobilized soldiers were looking for good jobs and college educations as guaranteed by the GI Bill. The affluent were moving to Florida and California. Immigrants were pouring in from the D.P. camps of war-torn Europe, and migrant laborers were coming in by the thousands from Mexico. The overwhelming mood was one of unrestricted mobility, and identification papers were not part of the postwar mood. In those days, many drivers didn't even bother to carry or renew their licenses, much less voters' registration cards or fishing permits. It was the era before computers and credit cards, and in rural California in the late

67

1940s a library card or even a recent letter was usually sufficient identification in minor matters. In my case, I was always terrified that I would have to prove my new identity (beyond the name on my engraved belt buckle) or that a sweeping registration program might be introduced, but the problem simply never arose. To my good fortune I was somehow able to slip through the cracks of the system until December 1947, when an employer in San Francisco made me apply for a Social Security card. Luckily, by then, my English was good enough to bluff my way through the panic of the moment. But until then, I had to survive and stay free.

To do that, I knew I had to leave San Pedro soon. The longer I stayed in any community the greater the chances that I would slip up or be recognized. It was clear that I would not be able to smuggle myself aboard a freighter bound for South America; the docks were patrolled and a hand-over-hand climb up the huge mooring lines looked dangerous enough to make me reconsider. Besides, I didn't want to leave the United States. But by Christmas 1945 I felt it was time to leave San Pedro, and early one morning, just before New Year's, I did.

LIKE MOST AMERICANS without an automobile in those days, I traveled by bus. It was safe, efficient, inexpensive, and anonymous. One could travel from Los Angeles to San Francisco by Pacific Greyhound for the nostalgically low price of six dollars, and even the smallest, remote towns could be reached or, if necessary, fled. I really enjoyed traveling the rural West Coast by bus. Nobody asked your name when you bought the ticket, dress was casual, and you could be as withdrawn or talkative as you liked. If I did say something foolish or mispronounced words my fellow passengers might laugh good-naturedly, but the chances that a policeman would be riding among us were slim. I enjoyed the freedom of being able to get off at any small town that struck my fancy, working for a few days, and then moving on. Most of all I enjoyed watching the passing countryside, enthralled as I still am by the beauty and variety of rural America. It was hard to believe that I wasn't still on a POW train, and I often came out of my reverie to be startled that the bus wasn't filled with fellow German soldiers. It was the blue-collar means of travel, and poor people understand the moods of other poor people. Good jobs were scarce and money was tight, and if that tall, skinny Norwegian-fella with the cardboard suitcase staring out the window didn't have much to say—well, that was O.K.

And, as always, I didn't talk much, partly out of fear and partly to sit back quietly and learn everything I could. I found out about all kinds of survival tips: ways to save money, towns to avoid where drifters weren't welcome, and most important, where the jobs were. It was a real education for me. I learned that one could buy good work clothes at war surplus stores, or get an emergency meal at a Salvation Army soup kitchen, or arrange for a post office mailbox in lieu of a permanent address. Finally, they told me about a vast labor subculture—agricultural migrant workers—who moved up the West Coast following and harvesting the ripening crops. Everyone agreed that it was a hard life, but that it was honest, healthy work, with lots of travel, camaraderie, and free fruit. That was for me! But I probably would not have ended my highway odyssey for life as a migrant picker had it not been for a crisis.

It was mid-March 1946, and I had been on the road for almost three months. I got off the bus in a small town way up near Medford, Oregon, to earn some more travel money by doing odd jobs. I signed on as a lumberjack, topping and felling huge trees. It was a fearful kind of work, dangerous and exhausting, and despite every precaution I had an accident. Somehow I slipped and slashed the calf of my leg. There was no question that it was a nasty gash. I was losing blood and needed medical attention quickly. Everything happened so fast. The next thing I knew, someone was driving me to the local hospital. I was terrified at the prospect of answering dozens of personal questions and of having to account for my past medical records, but the sight of the tourniquet below my knee convinced me that I had little choice. They fixed me up, but I had to stay for two days. And for two days I lived in fear. What if they checked up on "Peter Peterson" or searched for his nonexistent medical records? What if I started speaking German while under medication or in my sleep? I had escaped only six months before and was barely capable of conversational English. Who knows what I might blurt out in a moment of pain? I finally became so worried about the increasing curiosity of the hospital staff that, recovered or not, it was time to leave. I simply discharged myself in the middle of the night and bolted. My instincts told me, correctly as I later learned, that the authorities were tightening the net around California. From the hospital, I hopped and hobbled to the ever-welcome bus station and boarded the first outbound to the Mexican border. It was a mad dash for freedom.

Two days later I found myself on the Texas side of the International Bridge at El Paso, staring across at Ciudad Juarez. I was poised on the edge of a life-changing decision. Was it time to leave America? On one hand, the hospital might well have alerted the authorities, and the FBI could already be closing in on me. I knew the hospital was a dangerous idea from the beginning but had no other option. I wanted badly to remain in the United States, but not if it meant arrest and deportation. Besides, Mexico wouldn't be so bad. I wouldn't be a fugitive over there, and could even go back to being Georg Gaertner. Eventually, if necessary, I could learn to speak Spanish. The image of palm trees, beaches, and pretty señoritas beckoned to me from the other end of the bridge. Shoppers and tourists were strolling past me toward the bargains and naughty attractions of Juarez. I wavered as I tried to decide if I should join them and not return.

But what if the hospital hadn't reported me to the FBI? What if they had shrugged off the disappearance of the heavily accented "Norwegian" as just another ungrateful transient who couldn't pay his bill? Maybe I was still in the clear. And even if the hospital had reported their suspicions there was no reason to believe that the FBI would be particularly interested. Why would they connect "Peter Peterson" to an escaped German prisoner of war? Surely there were other suspicious-looking people in California. In any case, the FBI probably had their hands full with more dangerous criminals. Even if everything had gone wrong—if the hospital had reported me, if the FBI had taken the report seriously, if they identified me as the escaped POW, and if they considered the case a high priority—why would I take it for granted that they would catch me? California was a huge state, and I could change my name regularly. Hell, if I was cautious and kept moving they might never catch me! As I looked across at Mexico, foreign and intimidating in the evening darkness, I made my decision. I would stay in America and take my chances. I never looked back. Nearly forty years later I still consider that moment on the bridge the wisest decision I made in America.

ONCE HAVING DECIDED to remain, there was no question in my mind where I would live: California, of course. I worked for a few days in El Paso to earn my bus fare and caught the next Greyhound to the West Coast. But where in California was I headed? I knew I couldn't go back to San Pedro; that would be pushing my luck. I also realized that I wasn't ready for the hustle of Los Angeles or San Francisco. I was still too unsure of myself. Then I remembered the many conversations I had heard about the migrant workers—the earthiness, the constant movement, the freedom —and made up my mind to join them. My destination was Fresno, midway up the center of the state on the edge of the lush San Joaquin Valley. What fun! I was off on a new adventure. And the FBI would certainly never look for me in the migrant camps of northern California and Oregon. Nor would the migrant workers be particularly concerned about my past. I figured that as near-nomads, they didn't stay in one place long enough to catch up on world events or read about escaped POWs in the newspapers. From the conversations I overheard on the buses, many were probably running from the law themselves. If anything, they might even protect me. Fresno it would be.

In one of those great ironies of life, the bus route took me up US-10, which cut across the southwest corner of New Mexico toward Tucson, Phoenix, and San Bernardino: that route took us directly by Camp Deming and Camp Lordsburg! I couldn't believe it, but there it was on the wall map at the bus terminal in El Paso. I recalled being transported from the base camp to the branch camp at Deming on just such a highway, but it was too far away and too heavily trafficked to be considered an escape route, so I had put it out of my mind. Now, here I was, rolling past on a sleek Greyhound bus. Talk about being brazen! Would I wave? What if the bus stopped for passengers? What if a guard or camp administrator climbed aboard? It had only been eight months since I left, after all, and someone might easily recognize me. Still, I had no choice and, in fact, the trip was anticlimactic. When we passed the camps I scrunched down in my seat and barely shifted my gaze outside. I couldn't see Camp Deming beyond the mesa and later learned that it had been dismantled some months earlier when the POWs were shunted to Lordsburg and sent on to Europe. Those men destined for towns under Soviet control were, indeed, turned over to the Russians. Had I not acted when I did, I would surely have been among them. I did see Camp Lordsburg in the distance, however, and was relieved that the bus didn't stop to pick up any new passengers. The trip was otherwise uneventful, and I spent much of the time reliving my escape and congratulating myself on my daring and success. I had saved myself. I had survived the first few months, my English was improving, and I was off on yet a new adventure. Good going, Georg—uh, Pete.

IF ONE COULD compress the essence of California agriculture into a single sentence, it would be that "Farming in California is a business and not a way of life." California produces more than 90 percent of all the grapes grown in America; all its raisins; all its lemons; all the olives; prunes;

avocados; figs; almonds; artichokes; and a substantial percentage of the country's oranges, peaches, pears, cotton, lettuce, asparagus, peas, and tomatoes. The point is that California is not only America's agricultural cornucopia, but that its crops are heavily labor-intensive. Most of the produce has to be harvested by hand, which creates a critical demand for a continuous supply of cheap labor. More importantly, the harvest times frequently overlap, which finds the cotton harvest in the San Joaquin Valley in the fall, for instance, competing for the same laborers required by the grape and tomato harvests. Add to this the perishability of most of the major California crops—peaches, pears, grapes, tomatoes—which means that workers must be mobile, flexible, available, and cheap. On one day the apricots are too green to be picked, and with a turn in the weather the crop must be harvested in a week or the entire acreage will spoil. The key to California's agricultural success (in addition to irrigation) was its quarter of a million migrant workers: Mexicans, Filipinos, and American refugees from the dust bowls and the Depression of the 'thirties. They are reviled and bullied, overworked, and underpaid—and God help the worker who whispered the word "labor union"—but without them the California farmers would go under.

Migrant worker families, usually with four or five kids, lived in poverty-stricken camps around Stockton, Sacramento, Fresno, Bakersfield, Modesto, and Lodi, and moved with the seasonal requirements of each crop. Most were "Okies" from the pages of John Steinbeck's *Grapes of Wrath*, poor but honest folks living on the edge of subsistence. The pay was good when one could get it, but the harvest season was erratic and ever-moving, and unemployment was the rule for most of the year. It sounded like a hard life, but an interesting adventure—and a perfect place to hide.

OUTSIDE FRESNO I met a family of migrant workers who had just arrived from Arkansas. Like so many before them they came to California for a new start, driven by a lifetime of poverty and hard luck. His name was Dennis Whiles, about six feet tall, thin, with skin like worn saddle leather and several missing teeth. The "Missus" was short and stout, weather-beaten like her husband, whom she always called "D.W." and from whom she was never more than ten feet away. You could tell that they had been together for a lifetime and had been molded by the same tribulations. They had several boys, lively youngsters with old-looking eyes, and a shy pretty daughter of about eighteen. It was a picture of the Great Depression: torn and faded blue jeans and washed out print dresses. But what a wonderful family—a testimony to family life and the ability to survive. They took me in (I think they hoped to find a husband for their daughter) and for weeks at a time I became part of their family. We followed the harvests all the way up the San Joaquin Valley to the apple and cherry orchards of Medford, Oregon, and back. They gave me a corner of their one-room rented shack, partitioned by blankets and clothesline, and set a permanent place for me at the dinner table. They never pried into my past. My daily wages went into the coffee can like everyone else's and on and off for almost six months I was part of a family.

It was a difficult life. As early as 2 A.M. or 3 A.M., caravans of decrepit pickup trucks and buses, representing dozens of local farms, pulled into the middle of our camp to recruit workers. Contractors, producers, drivers, and foremen circulated among us describing the job, rate of pay, condition of the fields, and the distance from town. Some selected their workers based on skill and experience; others chose only family units or single workers; still others took all comers. Some trucks had the wage rates chalked on the side, often scribbled over by the comments of previous workers. As each truck filled with stretching and yawning workers pulled away, another moved up to take its place. Every day was different. Sometimes we worked like mad, stooping and cutting, for only five or six dollars per day; other times we were paid as much as fifteen or eighteen dollars.

I often went off on my own, sometimes for weeks at a time. I would team up with a couple of guys who were on their way to harvest citrus in Corcoran, and when that job was finished, I'd join up with some men going to prune pears at Bear Creek Orchard in Medford. It was a tumbleweed existence. I went wherever there was work and seldom remained in one place for more than the few days necessary to bring in the crop. Somebody would mention that laborers were being hired in some distant town and off we went. I rode the rails and lived in boxcars. I slept in trucks and bunked with strangers. Many evenings after work we'd sit around a campfire or on somebody's front porch talking or joking. Often there'd be a guitar or fiddle and we'd sing the Dust Bowl songs of Woodie Guthrie. One in particular that I still remember said that California was like a Garden of Eden, and that it was like heaven to live in and to see, but whether one believed that or not he'd find it wasn't so hot, if he hadn't some Do-Re-Mi. We sounded like dogs baying at the moon and laughed when we finished, but we all knew how true it was.

A curious feature of the work required that I travel with others, a habit that encouraged me to learn to develop new friendships. It was safer, of course, to travel with a buddy, someone who would guard your belongings while you slept. Most workers traveled in pairs. It was also economically sound since employers tended to hire men in teams rather than loners. There was an additional advantage in my case: my buddy would do all the talking and wage negotiations. That way no one would have a reason to ask me questions that I might not be able to answer. While there were occasional problems, such as when my companions would drink up my wages or shortchange me, it was still better than the risks I would be taking on my own.

Although it was still many years before the government or union organizers took an interest in the plight of migrant workers, an occasional social worker would appear in a camp or on the job to offer assistance. One such social worker, a redheaded woman named Jean Bergmann, was a frequent and welcome visitor to the migrant camps around Fresno and Visalia. Mrs. Bergmann drove her old dusty Chevy to godforsaken places like Dinuba, Kingsburg, Lindsay, Porterville, and Delano to provide county aid to needy families. She appeared in almost every migrant camp I lived in, though I never met her personally. It was almost twenty years later, when I was a successful American businessman and actually met her for the first time, that I realized how often our paths had previously crossed.

As the summer progressed, the Whiles family and I joined hundreds of other families who moved north toward the apples of Oregon. Farmers and ranchers often provided cabins and shacks for the "regulars" (like us), while others had to sleep in their pickups or cars. One of my sharpest recollections of that summer of 1946 is picking cherries. The cherry trees were enormous, perhaps twenty or twenty-five feet high and nearly as wide. Rows and rows of them, acre after acre. The ranch foreman would distribute empty boxes and assign rows to each worker. Each person was issued a long and heavy extension ladder, and the work began. Up and down the ladders we raced, reaching perilously for the ripest fruit at the top, and moving the ladders in a circle around each tree until it was picked clean. Then on to the next tree. It was back-breaking work, and a bit dangerous, which left me with a lifelong respect for the fruits and vegetables that supermarket shoppers take for granted. I remember working at one small farm where we were required to sing continuously, the song being unimportant. The moment we stopped singing, the foreman knew we were eating the fruit and came on the run.

However interesting the lifestyle, it was the closeness of family life that I enjoyed most. It had been more than six years since I left home in Schweidnitz, and I hadn't realized how hungry I was for stability and family intimacy. It was wonderful to relax and not worry whether I said something that might give me away. Here no one cared. I could mispronounce words or withdraw from the conversation and nobody was concerned. They treated me like their eldest son. At the same time, I enjoyed the role of the eligible bachelor although I was as embarrassed as their constantly blushing daughter at the dinner-table references to our possible marriage. Everyone knew that we had never so much as held hands, but the opportunity for laughter and merriment was too rare in the squalor of the migrant camps for me to take offense. For more than six months, on and off, I was part of a family again, and still recall with fondness the evenings I spent reading week-old newspapers while the boys joked or Dennis and his "Missus" talked about their experiences in Arkansas.

It was also another period of education for me. First came a new vocabulary: words like "piece work," "freewheeler" (a worker who traveled without his family), "Texican," (a Texan of Mexican descent), and "gate-hire" (the employing of workers who arrive unscheduled at an orchard and are hired on the spot). The occasional periods of unemployment also provided me with an opportunity to spend long hours in the Stockton Public Library. I read about American history, art, travel, language. I studied maps and devoured "how-to" books. I read any book or article that I thought might help me continue eluding the authorities and became a devotee of spy novels, Raymond Chandler thrillers, and Ross McDonald adventure stories. If I were to name three books that influenced me the most, however, I think they would be Constantin Stanislavski's *An Actor Prepares,* Machiavelli's *The Prince,* and Norman Vincent Peale's *The Power of Positive Thinking. The Prince* explained the complicated nature of Man's ambitions, and Machiavelli's advice to his prince benefited me as well. Stanislavski's book, still a bible to serious actors, coached me in the art of being someone else; and *The Power of Positive Thinking* convinced me that I could do it. Those three books were instrumental to my "success," and my two grown children, Lynn and Mark, will now know why they were so often asked to read them.

I settled into the routine of migrant labor and family life with the comfort of several new conclusions. First, I realized that I was temporarily safe. Even when I made such jarring slipups as the morning I sleepily answered a fellow worker's "Hi!" with an equally loud *"Heil!"* (which, mercifully, the Mexican workers in my truck didn't seem to notice), no one was particularly concerned. I had some breathing room to more carefully shed my old German identity while becoming a good American. Secondly, I realized that I needed human contact. Though I prided myself on my ability to survive on my own, to be a "loner," I longed for the warmth of family life. I was convinced more than ever that my own parents were dead or imprisoned and I terribly missed not having a home. I knew that I would soon have to venture out of my shell and make some close friends. Perhaps girlfriends, I thought enthusiastically. Someday I might even consider getting married, though the dangers of such a move far outweighed any benefits. Still, it was a sobering realization to find that I needed close relationships, but comforting to think that however risky, a nation of potential friends were out there for the asking. My final conclusion was that it was time to discard "Peter Peterson." It was too foreign, too unimaginative. The Norwegian cover story had served me well for the past year, but, now that my English had improved and my confidence bolstered, it was time to choose a more "American" identity. Something that would give me more substance. Stanislavski had taught me that the actor must "feel" the identity he is assuming; he must make each nuance of behavior second nature. I knew who I would become! Someone whose habits and viewpoints I was familiar with, and someone I could respect. When I left the migrant labor camps in November of 1946, I left "Peter Peterson" behind, and became Dennis Whiles. With some exceptions from time to time, I have been Dennis Whiles for most of my adult life.

Sometimes I feel guilty about taking Dennis's name. He never knew, of course, and I doubt if our records ever crossed as a result. I have my own Social Security number as, I presume, he has his, so our taxes were never confused. Besides, there must be hundreds of people with the same name, though I concede that I have never met another Dennis Whiles. Unlike primitive tribes who believe that taking their photographs in some way steals their souls, I don't think that I harmed Dennis by taking his name. In fact, I have always viewed my periodical borrowing of someone's name as a gesture of respect. It sounds self-serving, I know, but it's true nonetheless. I could never enjoy using the identity of someone I disliked, now could I?

Still, every now and then, I feel a slight tremor of guilt. Perhaps it's just nostalgia for my lost youth.

IF I FELT safe during 1946, it was not entirely due to the anonymity of the migrant camps. It turns out that I had a reprieve of sorts during most of that year. As a result of the Freedom of Information Act, I recently obtained my entire FBI file (weighing nearly five pounds) as well as that of the U.S. Army; and have had the rare treat of following the day-by-day activities of my hunters. What fascinating reading! I learned how often my surges of self-confidence and safety were justified, when the authorities were looking elsewhere. Other times they were within twenty miles of me and closing, and only my instinct to bolt—call it the intuition of the hunted—helped me elude a swoop by the FBI. Most interesting, perhaps, was the discovery that bureaucratic red tape and the lethargy of the FBI allowed me to pass my first and most vulnerable year in relative safety.

But, oh, how close those first months. Both files describe in detail the pandemonium that erupted the moment I escaped on September 22, 1945. A bed check later that night revealed that I was gone, and all hell broke loose. The commanding officer at the nearby Deming Army Air Base sounded the alarm, and the U.S. Army Provost Marshal's Office, the U.S. Customs Service, the U.S. Border Patrol, the Immigration and Naturalization Service, the Southern Pacific Railroad Police, and the El Paso County Sheriff's Office were mobilized to action. Each agency then mobilized its own units and the search was on! Dozens of my fellow POWs were questioned by the military authorities to find out my plans, my state of mind, and my destination. Luckily I hadn't discussed my escape with a soul, so there really wasn't anything they could say. Since it was well known that those of us from East Germany were to be sent back to the Russians, the Army concluded from the beginning, to my great advantage, that I had escaped to avoid repatriation rather than to commit sabotage or seek vengeance for our having lost the war. Consequently, I was not categorized as "Dangerous," a label that would have greatly intensified the search and might have provoked a nervous policeman to shoot first and ask questions later. My few belongings were searched for some clue to my destination: was I headed over the Florida Mountains to the Mexican border only forty miles south? Could I have decided to hitch a ride to the International Bridge at El Paso, about one hundred miles further? Perhaps I was enroute to Norfolk or Savannah or New York to hop a freighter bound for my native Germany? Maybe, the authorities speculated, I had "gone to ground," and decided to hunker down in nearby Lordsburg or Las Cruces until the heat died down, after which I could move about in relative safety. Curiously, they settled on the latter. I was somewhere in the area, they decided, probably hiking across the New Mexican desert "as I was trained to do in the Afrika Korps." Ironically, they never seriously considered the possibility that I might have jumped on the train that passed so close to our camp. Whatever their reasoning, the authorities concentrated their immediate energies on the New Mexican desert around Deming, which enabled me to make good my escape. Had they focused on the train, they could have wired ahead to any large town, and I would certainly have been found and arrested. Instead, my description was flashed to the New Mexico State Police, the Dona Ana County Sheriff's Office in Las Cruces, the Sierra County Sheriff's Office in Hot Springs, the Grant County Office in Silver City, and the Hidalgo Office in Lordsburg.

The Army's Provost Marshal's Office detailed thirty MPs in cars and jeeps to patrol the area between Deming and the border crossing at Columbus, and as far east as Las Cruces and as far west as Douglas, Arizona. And that was only the beginning. The commanding officer at the Deming Army Air Base dispatched three airplanes that searched approximately two hundred miles in all directions from the camp. Their weary-sounding reports in my files state that they returned with "negative results." On Sunday, September 23, the authorities sent out a posse of fifteen cowboys on horseback and they covered the area from Rodeo, New Mexico, to the Mexican border. Again, wearily, "with negative results." After several more days of "negative results," the Army brought in the FBI but I was already in San Pedro.

Curiously, the FBI did not maintain the pace set by the Army and the local authorities. Most likely they had more important cases to worry about, considering the growing Cold War and America's increasing concern about Soviet espionage. The fact that I was not labeled "Dangerous" made all the difference in the world, although the files contain some somber interdepartmental memos about the "espionage potential" of my "fluency" in English. Luckily for me, the agent in charge of the El Paso office decided that there was no evidence to believe that I would use my "fluency" for any other reason than continued flight to my destination. Had he concluded otherwise, the FBI most surely would have acted more quickly and I wouldn't have had that year to develop my new American identity. Lucky, indeed. As a result of the FBI's reluctance to continue the frantic pace set by the Army and the local law enforcement agencies, the government did not issue a wanted poster for a year and a half following my escape. A year and a half. What luck! The Army requested the distribution of a flyer as early as October 5, 1945, and the FBI refused. A second request on January 24, 1946, was similarly denied. I was fortunately not dangerous enough. Instead, the FBI shifted responsibility to the Army, noting that since I was probably headed back to Germany, U.S. intelligence teams in Europe should be assigned to monitor my friends and relatives. Checking the Army records for the same period, the intelligence teams were indeed dispatched, as were agents from the German Search Service *(Suchdienst Zentrale)* in Munich, and every imaginable person I ever knew was interviewed for information. In America, FBI disinterest continued until the Special Agent in charge of the El Paso office, one R. C. Suran, conveyed his annoyance to his superiors by noting that the "investigation conducted relative to this case has failed to reflect that this subject's re-capture is imminent." In layman's terms the message was: "we're not getting anywhere on this case—let's start taking it seriously." Even with such prodding from his own Special Agents, J. Edgar Hoover waited until February 14, 1947(!) before ordering the printing and distribution of a wanted poster for Georg Gaertner. Copies were sent to every post office and federal building in America, and as though discovering the case for the first time, Hoover personally ordered my apprehension moved to a front burner. In a rare personally signed memo, he forwarded my description and five photos to all fifty-two FBI division headquarters, including Anchorage, Honolulu, and San Juan. That produced action! My records now bulge with the investigations of leads and reported suspects. I was reported to have passed through West Yellowstone, Montana, wearing a "drab-colored overcoat and a cap with earflaps." A number of hapless suspects matching that description were picked up, interviewed, and released. I was then "positively sighted" on a work gang for the Milwaukee Railroad in Selby, South Dakota, and every member of every work gang in the area was interrogated. The Bureau then ordered that the 600,000 pieces of mail which arrived after the POWs had been repatriated, warehoused at Fort George G. Meade, Maryland, be searched for any correspondence addressed to me. Perhaps they might contain a clue or reference to my escape plan. The FBI shifted into high gear, but it was too late. By not acting sooner, the FBI had allowed me to slip through the net into California where I had a year to learn to survive. In fact, by the time my wanted posters began to appear in the spring of 1947, I had already progressed through two stages in my metamorphosis: first as the Norwegian immigrant, Peter Peterson, and then the Okie drifter named Dennis Whiles. The FBI had lost the initial advantage but was moving aggressively to make up for lost time. I knew none of this, of course, and at the moment that J. Edgar Hoover was finally authorizing the distribution of my wanted poster in February 1947, I was working at the Central Lumber Company in Stockton and living quietly at elderly Mrs. Cochran's white two-story rooming house on Lincoln Street.

MOVING STACKS OF lumber all day was nothing to write home about, but life in Stockton brought me out of my shell. My English and self-confidence had improved mightily over the last year and the months spent with my migrant "family" convinced me that I needed people. Trishia Cochran must have sensed my vulnerability, for she kind of adopted me during much of that year. We spent long evenings sitting at the kitchen table talking about her native Texas and recollections of early Stockton and the Bay Area sixty miles west. She explained where the jobs were to be found and how to keep them. It was obvious that I was a foreigner, despite my silence on the matter, but she never pried. We talked about art and economics, politics and friendship. We read the newspaper together every evening and she explained the nuances of journalism and the cryptic language of classified ads ("Fr rent: 3 rm apt w/bdrm, 2nd flr., pvt. bthrm, sep. entrance, $75/mo."). She also encouraged me to make friends, something I was hungry for but too frightened to attempt, and often insisted that her daughter, Beverly, a schoolteacher, include me when she went to parties, auditorium dances, and Saturday afternoon matinees with her friends. Beverly, a redhead like her mother, was lovely. She helped me blossom socially and taught me the proper dating etiquette. I laugh when I think back at how little I actually knew about social relationships, romantic and otherwise. I had had a few "liaisons" in the past, mainly carousing with my army buddies during our long stays in Italy and Greece enroute to North Africa, but I was too apprehensive to attempt anything since my escape. Whenever the opportunity seemed to present itself, outside of the gaudy bars of Beacon Street in San Pedro or during my bus travels around rural California, I froze. Part of my hesitation was the paralyzing anxiety that every young man experiences when first faced with the opposite sex, and part was my terror of discovery. Would my inexperience give me away? What if I said something that might alert the young lady to call the police? She might ask me questions about my past, my school years, my "major," or "the prom." I didn't have the ability yet for small talk and was as worried about my social awkwardness as I was about my sexual inexperience. Still, it was time to paddle out into the deep water, and for much of 1947, Beverly tried to "domesticate the stray" who had dropped into her life.

One of our most enjoyable pastimes during that year was tennis, and we spent much of our free time on the courts in Stockton. Now here was something that I was good at! More than that, tennis allowed me to mingle with people without having to carry on lengthy conversations or in any way account for my still-halting English. I found that my tennis skills came back amazingly fast, though it had been almost seven years since I had competed in championship tournaments in Germany. I went out to the courts every chance I had, often two or three times a week. Soon I had a circle of friends, including a fellow my age named Bill Techner, I remember, who looked enough like me to be my twin. We all began the tradition of meeting afterward for drinks, and my days as a recluse were over. I was becoming a social butterfly and quickly grew to enjoy the interdependence of trusted friends and the availability of good-natured fun. It was like having a large but comfortably distant family. They were like cousins, perhaps, though people came and left during the year. I felt protected. In the many years since those days in Stockton, I have enjoyed being surrounded by groups of friends, and always miss their friendship when I feel it's time to leave.

My rediscovery of tennis was exhilarating and developed into a lifelong passion. On various occasions I have been a tennis instructor and a racquet club owner, a tournament player and tournament referee. I have played doubles with movie stars and participated in an exhibition match with the legendary Bill Tilden. Yet, for all of the public exposure I have never been anxious about my safety while on the tennis court. I'll play my heart out before a cheering crowd and shake like a leaf as soon as I step off the court. I only recall one or two occasions when reality followed me onto the tennis court and the sight of sports reporters and photographers waiting on the sidelines convinced me to purposely lose the championship matches to avoid the publicity.

On one occasion, I thought I was finished. I was the tennis pro at the posh Aptos Country Club, near Santa Cruz. Coming out of my tennis shop I bumped into a man who had employed me twenty-five years before, Joe Chinchiolo, a man with whom I had worked side-by-side for much of the summer. We both stood dumbstruck at the sight of the other: I, frozen with fear, and he, with bewilderment. We both mumbled "Hi" as I watched him search my familiar face for a sign of recognition. He looked from the face of "Peter Peterson" to the name tag that read "Dennis Whiles, Tennis Director." We smiled and stammered for a few seconds, after which he turned on his heel and walked into the clubhouse. He seemed terribly hurt. We avoided each other for his remaining days, though I expected the police to arrive at any moment. I almost fled, but miraculously, nothing happened and life returned to "normal." Despite such close calls, tennis, like skiing, has been an emotional haven and a source of friends, good health, and occasional livelihood. That I recently won the Honolulu Kings Court Tennis Championship at the zesty age of 60 attests to the attraction and benefits of the sport.

At the end of 1947, however, I was growing uncomfortable in Stockton. I had changed jobs from the Central Lumber Company to the Wonder Department Store and then to the Continental Can Company, and I realized that it was time to change from Stockton. I left without a word and headed for San Francisco.

I CAN STILL remember my first vivid impressions of San Francisco that November in 1947. From the moment I stepped off the bus I was enthralled by the diversity of cultures, the dense fog that condensed and dripped off the trees in Golden State Park, the hilly streets, and the endless rows of "little boxes"—identical houses each painted a different color—that lined the surrounding slopes. I'll bet I've walked every side street of the city over the years and, like millions of tourists every year (as Tony Bennett croons), "I left my heart in San Francisco." After renting a cheap, dingy room on 19th Avenue, I set off to find a job. Passing the famous Clinton's Cafeteria on the corner of Powell and Market (today a Woolworth's store), I saw a sign in the window advertising for a busboy/dishwasher and quickly found myself employed. Clinton's Cafeteria was a monstrous place that held more than one thousand people. There was continuous activity as steady lines of people moved down the one-hundred-foot double buffet pushing fiberglass trays heaped with plates of food toward the big roast beef and ham at the end of the line. It was the picture of America: abundance, noise, and informality. It was a frenzied place to work. The restaurant's success rested on fast turnover, which meant that an army of busboys had to fan out among the tables and clear away the dirty dishes to prepare for the next wave of hungry diners. For the next two months I saw more dirty dishes, half-empty water glasses, and gravy-stained cloth napkins than most people do in a lifetime. While I was always alert for the possibility that someone, in all that traffic, might recognize me, I was working at too furious a pace to worry.

The job had several redeeming features, however. I didn't have to carry on a conversation with any of the customers, and there were a number of available exits if I suddenly had to bolt. The assistant manager, a twenty-eight-year-old ladies' man appropriately named Romeo, was a welcome distraction from the routine. Every morning Romeo stumbled in red-eyed and we gathered about him in breathless anticipation to hear the lurid stories of his most recent encounters. We often stood with our fingers in our mouths as girls came by to pick him up after work, and when different girls dropped him off in the morning. He willingly dispensed romantic advice and, being the same age and lonely for companionship, I was anxious to learn. I confess that despite his detailed coaching and encouragement, I was singularly unsuccessful. Romeo even arranged some dates for me, but I simply didn't seem to have the necessary polish and glib talk to maintain their interest. A few times he became so exasperated that he actually invited me to double-date—a rare learning experience, we all knew—but still to no avail. Eventually, Romeo wrote me off as a hopeless case.

The last major benefit in working at Clinton's, of course, was the food. How I ate! In fact, I was attacking a lemon meringue pie when the manager came over to me in the employees' dining room and dropped some papers on the formica table in front of me. "Fill these out," he said authoritatively. I had no idea what the forms entailed and the expression behind his steel-rimmed glasses offered little sympathy. I made out the words "U.S. Government" and "Social Security" as I stuffed the papers in my jeans and promised to return them the next day. The rest of the day was a blur, and all I could think about were the forms in my pocket. What should I do? This was the moment I had always dreaded. If I filled out the official application and was caught, I would be compounding my escape charge. How could I not be caught? And if I didn't fill out the forms the manager might get suspicious enough to call the police. If I broke and ran, as every instinct in

83

my body cried out to do, they would surely alert the authorities anyway. I returned to my little room on 19th Avenue and anguished about my future. Slowly I started to fill in the blanks, not at all sure that I would even turn it in when I was finished. Name: "Dennis Whiles." For my parents' names I decided to keep their real first names, Paul "Whiles" and Emma "Whiles," and added the English translation "Gardner" as my mother's maiden name. Laboring well into the night with half-truths and half-lies, I managed to fill out the papers. I listed all our birthplaces as "New York City," a metropolis of eight million people as far from San Francisco as possible. My education came from the plausible but nonexistent "Connecticut School for Boys," and my military service was listed only as "4-F: Unfit for service due to poor health." I figured that it would take the government several months to check the accuracy of my application. By the time they discovered that no such person existed, I hoped to have saved up a couple of hundred dollars and be long gone. With trembling hands I handed the manager my completed papers the next morning and began planning my escape. Why hadn't I crossed over into Mexico when I had the chance? For the next few days I moved through my shifts like a robot, expecting to be called in to the manager's office at any moment. What kind of story could I give him when my forms came back unprocessed? What if the FBI was waiting in the manager's office when I walked in? I couldn't believe that I had been so stupid as to fill out those damn forms. Now they had me! My evenings were already spent poring over road maps and bus schedules when one day after work I returned to my room to find an official-looking letter under my door. To my soaring relief, I opened it to find my Social Security card!! I had somehow slipped through the net once again! I was now officially "Dennis Whiles!" Finally I had some real identification in case I was stopped for a minor infraction, always a possibility in a large city like San Francisco. Best of all, it gave me the self-confidence to further expand my social circle and to explore other hobbies and sports.

If I felt particularly overconfident it was only because I didn't know how close the FBI was. At the time I was relishing my new official identity and actually looking forward to paying my taxes (which I felt would help me if I was eventually caught), the FBI was combing the nearby communities of Los Altos and San Jose for two unfortunate suspects who matched my description. Los Altos was only thirty miles away! (In Europe, the Army was bearing down on my "girlfriend" in Germany, poor Maria Hoff, with whom I had spent one evening during a bombing raid in Saarbrücken

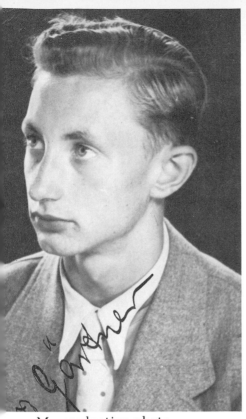

My graduation photo

With Alpine hat and leather coat

(below) The Gaertner family, 1940, before I went to war. From the left: my sister, Lotte; my mother, Emma; me; my sister-in-law; my father, Paul; my brother. Paul.

Playing tennis in Schweidnitz,
my home town, 1935

Ski talk, 1933

(left) The ski lodge
I frequented, 1933–1939

(right) Skiing,
mid-1930s

My boyhood friend Horst Trispel and I, 1938. I never saw him again after he entered the Army, though I heard he was a decorated combat officer and was later stationed in Paris.

At a Labor Service camp in Eastern Germany, 1939–40

As a 20-year old volunteer in the National Labor Service, I dug ditches in East Prussia. My sister, Lotte, saved this snapshot and my later military service photos, which I had mailed to my family.

(above left) Basic training in Ohlau, Silesia

(above right) With comrades on my promotion to Gefreiter, lance-corporal

(right) On maneuvers in basic training

(left) As a sergeant (officer candidate) in Rommel's Afrika Korps, 1943

(right) Officer candidate Georg Gaertner in dress uniform

(above)　Enroute to Greece aboard a cattle train at Christmas-time

(right) Bathing in the Adriatic Sea

(below)This Gypsy in Athens, 1942, predicted I would go on a "long trip."

(above) Boarding a Ju-52 tri-motor in Greece, 1942, on my way to North Africa

(below) My dugout near Tripoli, 1943. I am at right.

FEDERAL BUREAU OF INVESTIGATION
UNITED STATES DEPARTMENT OF JUSTICE
WASHINGTON, D. C.

F.P.C. $\frac{O \quad 31 \quad W \quad IIO \quad 20}{I \quad 28 \quad W \quad IOI}$

WANTED

GEORG GAERTNER, with alias: GEORGE JAERTNER

FBI No. 4,495,528

ESCAPED PRISONER OF WAR

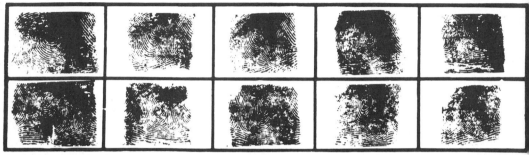

DESCRIPTION

Age, 26, born December 18, 1920, in Germany; Height, 5'11½"; Weight, 171 pounds; Eyes, blue; Hair, brown; Complexion, fair; Sex, male; Race, white; Nationality, German; Education, high school; Civilian occupation, draftsman; Languages, German and fluent English; Marital status, single; Scars and marks, scar on left index finger, dimpled chin.

Photograph taken in 1943.   Photograph taken August, 1943.

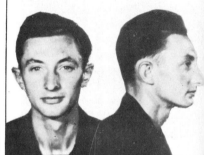

Georg Gaertner, a German Prisoner of War, escaped on or about September 21, 1945, from a Prisoner of War Camp at Deming, New Mexico.

Any person having information which may assist in locating Georg Gaertner is requested to immediately notify the Director of the Federal Bureau of Investigation, U. S. Department of Justice, Washington, D. C., or the Special Agent in Charge of the Division of the Federal Bureau of Investigation listed on the back hereof which is nearest your city.

IDENTIFICATION ORDER NO. 2099   (over)   Issued by: JOHN EDGAR HOOVER, DIRECTOR

As a weekend teacher on the Dodge Ridge Ski School Staff,
1954-55

Teaching "stretch" tennis near Hollywood and Vine, 1950

With my German "countess" friend

My friends (from left) Lowell Welch, Sidad's friend, Lowell's wife, and Sidad Serman.

As a sort of human St. Bernard dog, I was the first to reach the snowbound *City of San Francisco* streamliner stuck in Emigrant Gap in January 1952. In the bottom photo I am standing at rear.

(above) Although I never contacted my parents, they always kept a photo of me on the table. This was taken on Christmas 1956.

(below) Searching for anyone who might provide a clue to my whereabouts, my father ran this ad in major German and German-language American newspapers.

fayapaß teilnahm, ihren Bericht.

Fritz KOCH, Tecklenburg

Mein Sohn Georg geriet als Sturm-artillerist 1943 bei Tunis in Gefangen-schaft. Zuletzt erhielten wir Nach-richt von ihm aus Lordsburg, New Mexiko. Nach un-serer Ausweisung aus Schlesien hör-ten wir von einer amerikanischen Abwicklungsstelle, daß unser Sohn am 21. 9. 1945 aus dem Lager Lordsburg entflohen sei und bis jetzt nicht gefunden wurde. Viel-leicht weiß ein Kamerad, der mit ihm zusammen war, Näheres?

Paul GÄRTNER, Braunschweig

Foto · Privat

Georg Gärtner

(above) Herb Caen, beside me, never knew that I was the fugitive P.O.W. he once wrote about in his *San Francisco Chronicle* newspaper column.

(left) Standing beside tennis immortal Vic Seixas

(below) With screen star Robert Stack

(above) With Swedish tennis great Bjorn Borg (right) and his doubles partner

(below) With Lloyd Bridges at Aspen, 1984

(top) Painting Kaea Point from Maili

(middle) Jean and I at our pro shop

(left) In a bookstore, before I decided to commit my own story to print

(right) Jean and I, 1985

(below) My first meeting with Professor Arnold Krammer in a Houston hotel, January 1984. For four days I expected the FBI to walk in.

before I left for North Africa, and American and French occupation authorities were interviewing her regularly for some evidence of my location.)

Yet, despite my self-confidence, I decided to quit Clinton's. There were simply too many people there, and the chances that one of them might recognize me increased every day. I said goodbye to my friend Romeo, who was sorry to see his greatest challenge move on, and I caught a bus for the Sierra Nevada mountains. I went by Greyhound to Sacramento and from there up U.S. 40 toward Reno. An hour outside of Sacramento and we were in the mountains. Snow and pine trees and breathtaking beauty. The sunshine was almost blinding, and the air so crisp that your breath formed a misty cloud in front of your mouth and nose. The mountains around Schweidnitz were beautiful, to be sure, but this was sheer grandeur. I stared out through the frosted window at the snow-covered pine trees and the white mountainsides and slopes in the distance. I imagined myself skiing down the slopes, dodging between the trees, the powder flaring up around me, and the biting wind rushing past my face. I'd forgotten how much I loved skiing and realized that the decision to come up here was in response to some inner drive. I decided to look for a job at one of the ski resorts—not as an instructor, of course, since such prized positions went to the same people year after year—but perhaps as a maintenance man of some sort. Perhaps after a while, I could apply for a job on the slopes. If things worked out I could come back every winter. A regular. I could work at a ski resort during the winter months and follow the harvests or work at Clinton's during the rest of the year. In fact, with my new official Social Security card, I could work anywhere I wanted. Maybe it was time to stop being a dishwasher or busboy and begin looking for better jobs. Life held a limitless array of opportunities.

A hundred miles into the Sierra Nevada mountains, moving upward toward the Donner Summit and the hairpin turns that led to Reno, the Greyhound stopped for a break at the remote country store and post office at Norden. There was nothing there but a gas station and the bus stop. I struck up a conversation with the middle-aged couple that ran the station (they were Germans, in fact), and I learned that a ski resort was being reopened nearby called Sugar Bowl and that they might need a worker. I walked outside to think it over. I looked around at the snow paradise surrounded by Mt. Disney, Mt. Lincoln, and Mt. Judah, just below the seven thousand-foot peaks of the Donner Summit, in one of the remotest areas in the country. I was certainly safe here. I made up my mind. I told the driver to go on without me and started walking to the resort. As I came to the end of the road I saw the main lodge, a long wooden building with picture windows and a huge wooden porch, a smaller wooden chalet nearby, and a few houses scattered among the pine trees. That was Sugar Bowl in 1948, and my life was about to change again.

FOUR

S UGAR BOWL, TODAY one of the premier ski resorts of the Far West, was the creation of a man named Hannes Schroll. A champion-class skier in his own right, Schroll had married an heiress of the Union Pacific fortune prior to World War II, and together they set out to develop a top-quality ski resort. He picked one of the finest spots for snow conditions in California, attracted other wealthy stockholders (blue-blooded ski enthusiasts with names like Wellington Henderson, Donald Gregory, and Sherman Chickering), and designed a European-style winter paradise within easy reach of Reno (41 miles), Sacramento (90 miles), and San Francisco (190 miles). A Southern Pacific train left San Francisco at 9:00 P.M. and arrived at Norden at 7 in the morning, every day of the week. Sugar Bowl also boasted the first chairlift in California, awesome giant wooden towers that ran 3,000 feet from the peak of Mt. Disney down to the front windows of the three-story Tyrolean lodge building. It was not coincidental that Mt. Disney bore the name of California's great movie-maker; Walt Disney and his family were frequent guests, as were Holly-wood starlets like Jean Douglas and Janet Leigh. Above all, Sugar Bowl had spectacular skiing, and however whimsical the names of such runs as the "Pony Express Route," "49er Run," and "Donald Duck Schuss," some of the slopes were as perilous and exciting as any in the country. Imagine all this for the nostalgically low price of only $10 per day for a private room with bath, $1.25 for dinner in the rustic wood-paneled dining room, and 25

87

cents a ride for the ski lift. The skiers who came to Sugar Bowl in those early days were pioneers of a sport long before it became fashionable.

I trudged the six miles into the remote valley in December 1947 and walked into the lodge to ask for a job. I told the manager that I had been in the "restaurant business" and confidently flashed my new Social Security card. After some thought, he made me the kitchen fry cook. I was delighted with my new position, and while I sympathized with the digestive problems that the clientele was soon to experience, I was determined to do my best until an opening appeared for a ski instructor. Little did I know that my life would be intertwined with Sugar Bowl and the friends I made there for years to come.

I lived and worked at Sugar Bowl for the whole season: December to April 1948, and while I spent as much free time as possible on the slopes, the majority of my days were spent indoors with other members of the staff. First, there was Tim the bartender, twenty-eight years old and my new roommate. Tim was a sophisticated version of my friend Romeo at Clinton's. He was a snappy dresser with long sideburns a la Don Ameche and a perpetual cigarette in a long holder. Like everyone who worked at the ski resort, Tim's life was divided by the seasons. During the winter months he was our bartender, a witty raconteur of hilarious stories and naughty jokes. He was the master of the broad wink and the sultry stare. Women gravitated to him, as did we all. Some evenings he would be exchanging stories with the actor Robert Stack and his brother Jim at one end of the bar; dispensing financial advice to resort stockholders at the middle of the bar; and whispering seductively at the other end to some of the college girls who spent their Christmas vacations at Sugar Bowl. Tim was the hub of our social life. As soon as the snow began to melt and the last guests left for the season, Tim headed back to Hollywood and his budding acting career. I don't know how successful he became in the movie business, but he certainly had the charm, ambition, and good looks to become another Errol Flynn. Interestingly, as much as I envied him, I was taken aback when Tim once told me that his deepest wish was to become a skier like me. How curious are our dreams.

Another memorable character was Slim Mabury, a ski instructor for several of the local resorts. Slim was an appropriately thin, rawboned man of about forty, a southerner with a drawl you could cut with a knife. He reminded me of a cowboy who had somehow ended up in the wrong century. He was a top-notch skier, as comfortable on the slopes as he might have been on a horse, and even played the guitar (and yodeled!) for the guests on a Saturday night. Above all, Slim was a gracious man, almost cavalier, who never failed to invite me to his Saturday night songfests or introduce me to his friends as a "fellow instructor" and a "great skier." Coming from a real instructor, those were heady compliments in those days. Like Tim the bartender, Slim Mabury and I became fast friends. He took me under his wing and helped me get started in the ski world. "Any friend of Slim's is good enough for me," resort owners would often say when I later applied for jobs as an instructor or ski lodge manager. During the off-season, Slim worked as a park ranger and on one occasion helped me find a summer job. As luck would have it, the job ended badly.

He got me hired for the summer at the Ahwanee Hotel in Yosemite, in 1949 I believe, and things were rosy for the first several weeks. I arrived there by bus and was warmly welcomed as "Slim's friend." They put me in charge of maintaining some outlying resort cabins, and I found myself enjoying the work and the wilderness. One day I was approached by two men who furtively asked me aside for some questions. They introduced themselves as FBI agents and flashed their badges. For a few moments I thought I was going to faint. It was my nightmare come true. My heart was pounding so hard I barely heard them ask me about a woman whom they believed to be staying in one of the cabins; a nurse, as it turned out, who was suspected of stealing drugs from her doctor's office. I told them what little I knew and that she had checked out a long time ago. They thanked me politely and turned to leave. Then I saw them discuss something and turn to walk back toward me. If I looked nearly hysterical with panic, it apparently didn't show, because they simply asked to see her room. I handed them the cabin key with as much self-control as I could muster and excused myself to do some work. I calmly walked to the Ahwanee Hotel, packed my belongings, and left by a side door without explanation. I realized, of course, that they were not looking for me, but I couldn't control my panic. I was long gone before I calmed down. If they didn't know that I was a fugitive before, they probably knew it now. Why would an innocent person tremble and perspire because a couple of FBI men asked some routine questions about someone else? I decided that I had done the right thing by leaving when I did. I also decided that it would be unwise to stay in contact with Slim since the FBI might trace my relationship back to him. If the authorities made the connection between us, they might be watching for me to reappear. My discomfort at severing our relationship was compounded when I learned through mutual friends that Slim and his new wife "Squeaky" named their son after me! To young Dennis Mabury, today in his early thirties, I can only apologize for the embarrassment of learning that your godfather is a fugitive prisoner of war, and hope that your name has been a source of pride and good fortune until now. Interestingly, Slim and I reestablished contact the following year at Sugar Bowl and no mention was made of my behavior at the Ahwanee Hotel. He became a full-time park ranger in Moab, Utah, and used to drop me periodic postcards from exotic places like Mt. Shasta and Briele Canyon. Although my fear of the FBI seemed more than ample justification for my temporary disappearance, in retrospect, I wish that I had handled it differently.

Finally, there was Bill Klein. Wilhelm Klein and his brother Fred had emigrated to America from Vienna in 1938, and when I met him a decade later, they ran a successful ski school at Norden, California, that encompassed the University of California Lodge, the German Ski Lodge, the Sierra Club Lodge, and the Ski Inn Lodge (where Slim Mabury generally worked). Bill's brother had just left the ski business to become an airline pilot and Bill was casting around for a suitable assistant. He watched me do some impressive runs and offered me the job for the following season. What a coup! Not only did I have an assured instructor's spot for the next year, but I was part of an outstanding team. And Bill was a man after my own heart. He touched everything European in me (without knowing it, of course) and became my model for assimilation into the mainstream of American life (again, without knowing it). He was the most graceful skier I had ever seen, a Fred Astaire of the slopes, and I worked very hard to develop a smoothness of my own. Bill's wife, Helen, a beautiful blonde American, was the daughter of Berkeley's famous Professor Hildebrandt. She was the business brains who ran the ski shops, and he was the total skier. Under his expert guidance I became a "smooth" skier and a good instructor. He assigned me to his best clients: society people, business executives, and wealthy heiresses. In fact, after several seasons on the slopes I was becoming quite a star. I was almost thirty years old and in robust good health from constant skiing during the winter and migrant labor during the summer. My accent, which I worked so hard to get rid of, turned into a social advantage; ski instructors all seemed to have accents: Swiss, French, Norwegian, Austrian, German—who could tell one from the other? No one ever questioned my background. The only requirements of my job were that I ski like a champion and be able to teach others to do the same. The ability to teach depended on charm and understanding, traits that I was developing rapidly. Thanks to the tutoring by so many people along the way—Mrs. Cochran back in Stockton, Romeo at Clinton's, Tim the bartender, Slim Mabury, and now Bill Klein—I was becoming a glib talker and an outgoing social butterfly. Not only did my unfolding personality make me a good ski instructor, but the ladies began to notice me. I had finally arrived.

First there was Annie Elbert, whom I nicknamed Goldilocks, a member of the "Schneehasen" (Snow Bunnies) Ski Club from the University of California at Berkeley. Goldie was a baby-faced blonde, the proverbial poor-little-rich-girl whose ever-present problems ranged from guilt over starving children in Africa to the injustices of McCarthyism. Our romance blossomed to the point of meeting her mother in their beautiful home in the wealthy Presidio section of San Francisco before I came to my senses and gracefully bowed out.

Then there was the mysterious and sultry woman who introduced herself and was known to all only as a "German countess." Tim pointed her out in the bar at Sugar Bowl. She wasn't a regular guest at the resort, and I remember having to out-charm Mr. Schroll himself, there on one of his periodic visits, to get her attention. The result was a whirlwind romance that took us to the nearby gambling casinos of Reno in my Packard, gala floor shows starring Frank Sinatra and Ava Gardner, and a week at the Mapes Hotel that probably aged me ten years. One morning I awoke and "the Countess" was simply gone.

My last girlfriend during those first seasons as an instructor was Barbara Bigelow, an attractive divorcee who was the accountant-manager of the Soda Springs Hotel. Always dressed in austere black turtleneck sweaters and looking for all the world like Yvonne DeCarlo, Barbara and I (and her inseparable bad-tempered little black French poodle) spent our several weeks together dividing our time between the Soda Springs Hotel and the nearby Rainbow Tavern. She was the picture of sweetness until I forgot to show up for a dinner date. When I came over the following day, remorseful and apologetic, I was greeted by a barrage of invective, several slaps, and a biting dog. I decided not to pursue the relationship. In fact, that was my last romance for a while. I was getting tired of being a slave to my glands, and when my boss, Bill Klein, gently lectured me about professionalism, I conceded and tried to avoid such romances in the future. He was right, of

91

course. Although I would drift to other jobs and careers, Bill was always a good friend. I was gratified to recently learn that one of the most beautiful runs down the slope of the 8,000 foot Mt. Lincoln at Sugar Bowl is named "Bill Klein's Schuss."

In 1948, however, I was just the fry cook, making hamburgers for illustrious guests like Robert Stack, and enjoying my new-found friends. When the snow melted in April, I said goodbye to Tim, Slim, and Bill and headed for San Francisco. I decided to go back to work at Clinton's. Despite my periodic waves of paranoia at the possibility of being recognized by any of the many hundreds of people who came through daily, I knew the routine at Clinton's, the neighborhood and the management. I had at least one good friend, Romeo, who held my job for me. Anyway, it was back to Clinton's and the noise and the mountains of food. I worked there, without incident, for the next seven months, until the beginning of the ski season in December. Then I returned to the slopes of Sugar Bowl.

My FBI files indicate that on the very day that I began work at Clinton's a number of vigilant citizens spotted me in Milwaukee. On Saturday, March 6, 1948, the *Milwaukee Journal* had apparently carried a feature article about the German prisoners of war in America and mentioned several who were still at large. And, of course, there was my photograph. The usual crack pot calls poured into the offices of the local authorities. Several people reported that I had been regularly sighted in the neighborhood of 27th Street and West North Avenue; another report identified me as frequent drunk in a local tavern. The FBI, long without leads, mobilized an army of agents to interview neighborhood residents and the patrons of bars like Nick's Knickabob Tap on 26th and State with "negative results." Looking at my army files for the same period reveals that they were still bearing down on my poor "girlfriend" Maria Hoff. It was clear that once having lost the initiative immediately after my escape, the authorities were working in the dark and were anxious to consider any possibility. This time, thankfully, they were way off.

The remainder of the year at Clinton's Cafeteria was routine and uneventful—no close calls, no romances, no excitement. There was, however, an important change in my outlook. One of the benefits of working at Clinton's was my ability to take time off, as long as I cleared it with Romeo. I just didn't get paid, that's all. Sometimes I would take off for several weeks at a time, usually on a bus trip or to earn some money playing tennis. It was on one of those tennis trips that I found myself in Palm Springs. I applied for a part-time job at the very exclusive Palm Springs Racquet Club, which was owned, like much of Palm Springs, by a grand old lady named Mrs. McManus. She saw the Racquet Club as her private estate and took a personal interest in every facet of its management. She often walked the grounds, cane in hand, pausing only to chastise a gardener or grumble at a handyman. Still, everybody loved her. She looked me over, dismissed my claim to tennis skills with a wave of her hand, and decided that I was a custodian. After thinking it over, she expanded that to custodian and security guard. I took the job. She scrutinized my work for several days before allowing me use of the courts and eventually gave me permission to give lessons in my free time.

I had a wonderful time. I played tennis with the greats and near-greats. I spent an afternoon with the legendary champion Bill Tilden and crossed paths with eighteen-year-old Elizabeth Taylor. During my free time I watched Lucille Ball and Desi Arnaz rehearse at the fashionable Chi-Chi Club. Although I spent only part of the summer in Palm Springs, it was exhilarating. I saw the shops and the clothes and the cars, and discovered something about myself: I wanted to be rich. I wanted to enjoy the benefits of the luxuries around me. This was America, after all, the land of opportunity. It was almost unpatriotic to be poor in America. In my case wealth also meant security: rich people didn't go to prison or get deported to Eastern Europe. If I had enough money the authorities might think twice before making an example out of me; and if I had to flee, I could certainly move faster and farther if I had plenty of money. I don't know why it had taken me so long to "discover" the importance of money; perhaps the realization came with my growing self-confidence. Perhaps I was just overawed by the opulence of Palm Springs and the wealthy set. Whatever the reason, the possibility of making lots of money settled in the back of my mind from then on. (Fortunately, it never became an obsession as it had with so many people I met in life. Any single-minded drive toward such an elusive goal, I found, only keeps the person from enjoying the many other wonderful things along the way. It reminds me of people today who go around with those little Walkman earphones: they are so intent on listening to their music that they often miss the interesting attractions along their route. Worse, they may not hear the sound of an oncoming car. In my case, the mythical car might be filled with FBI agents.) I am pleased that my dreams of big money did not become my first priority, the more so since I did not accomplish it. Oh, I've made a bundle from time to time—once my wife and I lived an entire year in Hawaii without working—and when it's gone, we start again. Like millions of Americans, I was now always on the lookout for the perfect "gimmick."

I looked for things to invent. My first "flash" came only weeks later that summer as I was returning from Palm Springs to Clinton's in San Francisco. As my bus passed through Los Angeles, I began to notice, almost for the first time, the number of convertibles at every intersection. Looking down from my bus window I saw packages and bags of groceries in every car and began to wonder how to develop an easily adjustable top that would also protect valuables from being stolen. Clearly, a cloth top wasn't sufficient. I hit upon an idea that resembled a rolltop desk, something like the natural armorlike plates of an armadillo. When I got back to San Francisco, I spent my evenings in my rented room near Golden Gate Park, in an area that the natives call the "Fog Belt," designing my invention. I eventually sent the completed plans to General Motors (why not start at the top?), but several weeks later my plans came back unopened. An attached note explained that GM has its own research department and did not accept suggestions from the general public. Like every budding inventor whose ideas are rejected, I was angry at their shortsightedness and took consolation in the fact that they were the losers. It was a variation of "I'll-hold-my-breath-until-I-turn-blue-and-then-they'll-be-sorry-when-I'm-lying-in-my-coffin-and-it-will-be-too-late." After a few more rejections, however, I shelved that project and moved on to other ideas.

I came up with dozens of gimmicks, some more successful than others. Once, while learning to play golf in San Mateo, I was struck by the number of golf balls that had been abandoned in the large pools of what they call "casual water" on the fairway. Surely there would be a market for a device that could salvage the balls, and I came up with a small "grabber" that fit on the end of the golf club. I paid a local handyman to build a prototype and sent the model to a patent attorney. Some months and several hundred dollars later, I had my first official patent! I was elated and figured that I was on my way to the top. Unfortunately, I knew nothing about marketing. I didn't know how to get the golfing world interested in my terrific invention. Moreover, the next few seasons were bone-dry and whatever interest there might have been for a ball-retriever evaporated with the puddles of 1953.

I later tried to apply the same principle in the development of a baseball toy for children, something like the old paddle ball on a rubber band, but which allowed the player to catch the ball in a "grabber" device. I even advertised the toy on local TV but with little success. Those few that sold often came back with broken rubber bands. Eventually, I shelved that too.

My best invention—the one that would have made my fame and fortune—came out of left field. One winter day in 1951, I found myself sitting next to a charming gentleman named Howard Head. In those days resort guests to Sugar Bowl were brought from the Southern Pacific train depot at Norden by a tractor-drawn sled. He was coming to interest Bill Klein in his new skis, aluminum and plastic instead of the traditional wooden skis, and for more than half an hour he extolled the virtues of aluminum in modern sports equipment. I was convinced and so was Bill, whose ski shop decided to carry the new skis. I have the distinction of owning serial number 16 of Mr. Head's revolutionary skis. But more importantly, he had set my mind to considering other uses of aluminum in sports equipment. I decided to develop an aluminum tennis racquet. Thus began an odyssey that lasted more than a decade. First, I had to develop a prototype. That meant working late in the evenings with assorted lengths of aluminum tubing trying to figure out the ideal size of the racquet, the grip of the handle, and balance points. I paid a Swedish fellow in East Oakland to help me with the mold and the drilling of the holes. Then I began to search for a partner. I wanted someone to commiserate with and someone who could offer suggestions. If he also had money to help finance the idea, so much the better. One day on the tennis courts in San Francisco I met Mike Dorst, an invention enthusiast full of suggestions and encouragement. He also had enough money to indulge his interests. What started out, frankly, as a mercenary effort to find a well-heeled partner became a genuinely close friendship that lasted many years. That partnership was supplanted by another investor friend, a wealthy San Mateo real estate developer named Alf Karstens. The two of us spent endless hours analyzing the fine points of our "perfect" new tennis racquet. For every two steps forward, we slid one step back. Our efforts were complicated by the need for secrecy; we thought that if word got out hundreds of inventors would move in on my idea. In retrospect, I don't know why we were so concerned since we were surrounded by skeptics. Finally, when we were ready to approach a manufacturer, we hit a new snag: the strings were breaking. We traced the problem to rough edges in the drilled holes and many more months went by as we considered possible solutions. Ultimately the problem was solved by Alf's seventy-year-old father, working in his garage, who devised a better method of drilling the holes and presented us with a perfect model. We dubbed our revolutionary product the "Dennis Racquet." Yet, however revolutionary, we had to find a buyer and manufacturer, a frustrating odyssey that consumed the remaining six years of the decade. I spent years trying to convince sporting goods companies like Wilson and Head (Mr. Head poo-pooed the whole idea) that an aluminum tennis racquet was the wave of the future. Every inventor believes that his rejected ideas are simply too far ahead of their time, or that their invention threatened an established industry. In my case I think both are true. It was a marvelous idea, as more successful inventors were later to prove, but for more than ten years I rode an emotional rollercoaster, from the elation of correcting minor flaws to the depression of spending endless hours in the outer waiting rooms of cynical business executives. Once there was a rare success, but when Wilson finally broke down and ordered a respectable 100,000 racquets, but their price (in that case, $10 each) was simply too low to pay for our manufacturing. Over the years friends and financial backers have drifted in and out, and I've changed jobs and addresses with regularity, but the dream of becoming a millionaire with my aluminum tennis racquet is always at the back of my mind.

HOWEVER ENJOYABLE THAT short exposure to the luxuries of Palm Springs, I had to return to my normal life. I finished out the year at Clinton's and headed back to Norden for the snow season. My job with Bill Klein's ski school was waiting for me, though I was headquartered to the Sierra Club rather than Sugar Bowl. Slim was there, too. So was the "Schneehasen" (Snow Bunny) Club of giggling Berkeley coeds. The only jarring note was the presence of a lodge manager who had retired from the FBI! I gave him a wide berth, seldom saying more than "Hi" as we passed one another in the lodge. Otherwise it was a wonderful season. I was responsible for groups at the Sierra Club Lodge, Cal Lodge, and German Lodge, as well as at Sugar Bowl, and taught both Alpine downhill and cross-country skiing. I was beginning to feel comfortable, safe, and self-confident. I even bought a car: a beat-up 12-cylinder Packard limo from an attorney in Soda Springs. It cost me fifty dollars and only seemed to run on six of the twelve cylinders, but the dating possibilities that came with the car made my head spin. I dreaded the moment when I would have to sign the bill of sale, and actually closed my eyes to scrawl my name as illegibly as possible. I kept the car in an unused shed at the lodge and only took it out on weekends. It was great to be mobile, but I lived in fear that I might be stopped by the police. I didn't know the rules of the road, and, of course, I didn't have a driver's license. But was I popular with the girls!

As the season came to an end, it was time to consider a summer job. I was getting tired of Clinton's. It was just too noisy and too dangerous. Considering the number of people who passed through the cafeteria every day, the odds of being recognized were growing ponderously against me. I decided to look for different work when I returned to San Francisco. I could always take short jobs as a migrant worker or tennis teacher, but I needed a base of operations, a steady job. I returned to San Francisco in April and began walking the avenues in search of interesting employment. Just across Market Street, not far from Clinton's, was the Emporium, one of the best department stores in the city. The Big E, as the Emporium was called by most, was owned by the Capwell Department Stores of Los Angeles and boasted some of the most creative window displays on the avenue. I had often wandered through its five floors marveling at the quality of the merchandise and the artistry of the displays. Though I had no previous experience, I marched up to the display department on the top floor and boldly applied for a job. They made me an apprentice window decorator! What that boiled down to was a "go-fer": my job was to "fetch" the tools, carry the huge canvas backdrops, rearrange the display props, and so on. I loved being around creative people, though their lifestyles and relationships were often peculiar to me. Still, we all got along well. I was anxious again about my accent and tried to speak as little as possible. I think the fact that I was both cooperative and quiet made the eight months that I spent at the Emporium so much fun. Eventually I was even allowed to design my own display for the latest best-selling book in the window on Market. Personally, I thought it looked terrific, and strolled past the window many evenings to admire my handiwork. I did have a few disquieting moments, however, as I worked in the Market Street window: people often collected to watch me arrange the props, and I dreaded the moment when somebody who worked in a post office or police station might point with recognition and go for the police. However, my only close call that summer took place elsewhere.

Sometimes after work I would stroll through Golden Gate Park, listen to a free concert in the park pavilion, or enjoy the breathtaking exhibits at the de Young Museum. Once in a while I would go into a bar for a beer and conversation. That's where it happened, in a neighborhood bar on a Friday evening. I had been propped at the bar for about an hour, listening to the discussions and banter around me. Suddenly an argument erupted in a back booth. Several people were shouting at one another, and before anyone realized what the racket was all about, we heard two loud gunshots. Everybody crowded to the back to see what had happened, and we were still craning our necks when the police arrived. The police!! It had all happened so quickly. The next thing I knew everyone was instructed to remain seated, because the police needed our statements. An ambulance came and left, and the interviews began. Before we were allowed to leave, each patron was asked back to a booth where a detective took statements and particulars. By the time it was my turn I was sweating and my hands were shaking. The detective stared at me from under his snapbrim hat, smiled that bureaucratic smile, and began to ask questions: "Name and address?" "Place of Business?" "Age?" "How much have you had to drink?" "Do you come here often?" "In your own words, what happened here tonight?" I could barely understand his rapid-fire questions, much less answer them coherently. My name alone came out something like, "Uh, Dennis, uh, yeah, Dennis, uh, Georg, no, Whiles." By the time I stumbled through my address and my job at the Emporium, he was squinting with suspicion. When I finally finished my brief statement, he told me to wait by the bar for some additional questions. I moved numbly to the bar as instructed and overheard the detective tell one of the uniformed police to take me downtown for questioning. Panic set in, and I knew that if they started checking my story, I was finished. I must have looked pale enough to convince the uniformed officer that I had to make a stop in the bathroom, because he nodded understandingly and positioned himself outside the door. I locked myself in the men's room and looked desperately for some way out. The window! Like a trapped animal, I fought to open the grimy window and, with my heart pounding, I climbed out into an alley. It was like reliving my escape from Camp Deming. There was no train this time, however, and I ran twenty blocks to my rented room and sat in the dark for an hour until my hysteria subsided. For days I worried that the police would trace me, but they must have decided it wasn't worth it. It had been a close one.

WHEN WINTER ROLLED around, I left the Emporium and automatically headed back to the Sierra Club lodge. The old gang was there: Bill Klein,

Slim, the Berkeley snow bunnies, even the ex-FBI man who managed the main building. My old Packard was there too, up on blocks in a storage shed. I knew it was going to be a terrific season, and it was. I spent much of my time teaching cross-country skiing, a grueling sport that involves striding more than skiing. I much prefer the speed and powder spray of Alpine downhill skiing, but cross-country was in vogue and Bill was the boss. Little did anyone know that I had once instructed German recruits in cross-country skiing in preparation for the invasion of Russia. It turned out to be a fortunate skill to have practiced.

I had two romantic attachments that winter. First I took up with a young newspaperwoman named Dolores Chambers who wrote a respected column on farmer's market shopping areas for the *Sacramento Bee.* Dolores was a widow whose husband had been shot down over the Pacific, and it didn't take many weeks to realize that she was in the market for a new husband. We had a wonderful time that season: movies, restaurants, long talks, and drives in my Packard. We were becoming an "item," as they used to say in those days, and might have become even more serious were it not for two persuasive arguments. The first came in the form of another no-nonsense lecture from Bill Klein, always business, about my neglecting the other students. It was a quiet warning that continued socializing might cost me my job. The second argument against continuing the relationship was my own realization that I was attracted by her periodic references to marriage, home, and children. It sounded appealing until I realized that it could simply never be: I was a fugitive German prisoner of war and marriage was out of the question. I would be jeopardizing her as an accomplice and making myself too vulnerable. We parted good friends and she remained in my thoughts for many years.

As a result of Bill's warning, as well as the discovery of my own emotional vulnerability, my other relationship that winter was entirely platonic. In sharp contrast to the sultry and torrid romances of earlier seasons, my friendship with Carla Wolff was giddy and uncomplicated. Carla was one of those bubbly people who are enthusiastic about everything. She was seventeen, a lovely young lady from San Francisco who spent most of her school vacations at the lodge. Carla was a bundle of energy, always cheerful and flirtatious in a little-girl manner. Somehow we decided in the midst of a silly mood to make some funny ski training movies. I bought a secondhand movie camera, the kind with the wind-up key in those days, and we set out to make people laugh. In one of our training films. I dressed up like a clown, and in another I was the villain "Oil Can Harry" chasing Carla as the Damsel in Distress. Friends and guests would stand in as extras and shout suggestions from the sidelines. We made several serious training films and an action documentary about the yearly Silver Belt Race at Sugar Bowl. Then came the fun of editing and finally the choice of music scores for the background, such as the "Peer Gynt Suites" for the magnificent mountain scenes and "Malaguana" for the race. For one short feature we harnessed some of the new lodge manager's beloved Samoyed dogs, powerful Siberian-bred with thick white coats, to pull a dog sled in our "Sergeant Preston of the Yukon" rescue film. We were like brother and sister and while we continued to correspond after the season ended, the widening differences in our lives eventually saw the cards and letters end. I wonder what became of her, though; her cheerful attitude and boundless enthusiasm could only have produced a happy and productive life.

THERE WAS A far more serious event that winter; Bill had a very bad accident. It was one of those flukes that I suppose could happen to the best skier. Worse yet, it took place right in front of me. Bill was coming off the top of the mountain at the Sugar Bowl, down a perilous straight run called "Main Street," which ended at the base of the tow lift outside of the lodge. He was in a "show-off" mood for some of his friends, something which we all did regularly. I was at the bottom of the tow lift with a group of beginners and shaded my eyes to watch him start down from the summit. He was a marvelous skier and everyone paused to admire his dramatic run. People "oo-ed" and "ah-ed" as he worked his way down the slope at breakneck speed, weaving and shifting with the grace of a ballet dancer. Suddenly he came upon a group of intermediate skiers who were huddled at the top of their shorter run. He managed to avoid them but somehow lost control. We watched with growing apprehension as Bill fought to regain his balance. We were riveted with horror as Bill zoomed toward us at the base of the tow lift. Suddenly he hit the huge wooden telephone pole that served as the bottom of the tow lift, no more than ten feet from where I was standing. He hit the pole like an express train and flipped end over end like a sack of potatoes. We rushed him to the hospital at Truckee and waited anxiously for the diagnosis. Although he was lucky to be alive, the news was hardly good. Bill had a ruptured spleen and had sustained enough bone damage to require a silver pin in his hip. While he would eventually recover and return to the slopes as fine a skier as ever, Bill was finished for

100

the season. That, in turn, meant that much of the responsibility for ski instruction fell to me.

I loved the opportunity to get in more skiing and to teach the snow bunnies without a periodic lecture about professionalism, but my new responsibilities created new problems. The first was visibility. The more people I saw and the more group photographs that guests took home at the end of the season meant a greater chance of being recognized. It was getting chancey. The second problem was a question of salary. Bill was spending his recuperation time developing a string of ski shops at each lodge in the area, as well as a store projected for San Francisco (today located in charming Ghirardelli Square). In short, I was doing the teaching and he was getting most of the money. I liked and admired Bill, but how was I going to become a millionaire in America if I did the work for another man's earnings? While I considered my options, the Sierra Club's board of directors was independently growing self-conscious about the obvious inequity and voted to make me the head instructor at Norden. I had not initiated the board's decision but cannot state that I was unhappy with my new promotion or with the fact that I was now entitled to keep the money I earned. The new situation dampened our friendship for awhile, but Bill understood that business was business, as he himself often said. He later helped me get started when my wife, Jean, and I opened our own tennis pro shop at Aptos Seascape in 1970. Bill and his brother Fred were kind enough to advance us some much-needed merchandise from their store in Ghirardelli Square.

AFTER FINISHING OUT the season as the Sierra Club's new instructor, my immediate concern was to find summer work. Fortunately that year, 1950, the Sugar Bowl Corporation decided to replace the wooden tower chair lift, built in 1939, with new steel towers, cables, and chairs, and I got a job with the Colorado-based company that got the contract. I was assigned to help a grizzled old journeyman carpenter tear down the old wooden structures and dig holes in the side of the mountain for the new foundations. Those holes were much tougher to dig than the foxholes in North Africa. Anyway, one bright summer day we were putting the finishing touches on the legs of our new tower while another crew was stringing a steel cable up the hill. The old carpenter and I were busy pouring concrete into the gaps around the steel legs when he looked up the hill and told me to get the hell out of there. The cable had snapped loose at the top and was whipping downhill like a live three thousand-foot snake. My cohort scrambled behind some huge pine trees and was shouting for me to get away from the tower. I yelled back that I was safe where I was, standing beneath the four legs of the structure. I watched with fascination as the loose end of the steel cable created gray puffs on the ground like a giant rabbit coming downhill. At the last moment I decided to heed the advice of my partner and bolted for the trees. When the splice end of the steel cable arrived at our station, it kicked high above the tower and then whipped down beneath the legs of the structure. When the snake finally looked dead, we ventured out to find the unraveled end of the cable lethally embedded in the very spot where I had stood only moments before.

For hours I couldn't stop shaking at the thought of my narrow escape. As with any close call, one suddenly has a new appreciation of life. Then comes some serious thoughts about the future. There's nothing like a brush with disaster to make you take stock of things. My first conclusion was that I should have listened to the carpenter's warning. Staying put as long as I had, I now wondered if I didn't have the brains that God gave rocks. The second realization was that life was more transitory than I had thought and that it was time to begin planning some direction for my future. I was thirty years old and no closer to being a millionaire than when I was a sergeant (K.O.B.) in the Afrika Korps.

I decided to open my own ski school. There were dozens of little ski resorts in the mountains and national forests of northern California; any one of them would be happy to have an inexpensive ski instructor with top references. I certainly had those: several of my former students had gone on to receive skiing scholarships at major universities and one of my early prize students, Susie Chaffee, even made the U.S. Olympic team.

I heard about a small resort down near Jackson in the Eldorado National Forest that was looking for an instructor, and when the summer ended and the tower was completed I took a bus to a place near Peddler Hill. The owner was a short, feisty guy with gray hair who welcomed me with open arms. He had just finished building a small lodge and a dormitory for men and women and was grateful to find an experienced ski instructor. He told me to report back when the first snow came, and I did.

It turned out to be a short-lived success story. The resort was just too new; it had not attracted a following. In fact, most of the season I spent in the bars and gambling casinos of nearby Jackson. I did have one serious student, a woman in her late twenties who was working toward her doctorate in psychology at UCLA, and she was the reason I quit at the end of the winter. One day she confided to me that she was being hassled by some man at the lodge and begged me to sneak into her room in the dormitory to protect her from his persistent advances. I gallantly consented. Sure enough, as we sat whispering in her dark room there was a tapping at the door. A man's voice asked to be let in. I jerked the door open to confront the cad and found myself facing the owner of the resort! After we both regained our composure and exchanged a few inane pleasantries, we each returned to our regular rooms, but it was clear that my days at the resort were numbered. My relationship with the owner cooled considerably. Moreover, he evidently told his wife that he had caught me in the woman's room (never mentioning his part in the drama) and the old lady became nastier to me by the day. I never thought I would be glad to see the snow melt, but at the first signs of spring I packed my belongings, thanked them for my pay, and closed the "Dennis Whiles Ski School." So much for my first taste of business.

LUCKILY, I WAS willing to give business another try, since the next opportunity altered my life. I was approached that summer on the tennis courts in San Francisco by a dynamic giant in his mid-twenties named Herb Lipkin. His girlfriend, Georgette, had apparently taken skiing lessons from me and was impressed with my ability to talk to people. She recommended me as a possible salesman for his new business venture. Herb and his parents had owned Broadway Glass in Oakland for many years but some recent reversals had convinced them to branch out into a brand-new enterprise. They were introducing the pre-hung door. That is to say, doors were previously cut to order at the construction site and the hinges measured and adjusted by a carpenter. Doors generally required a carpenter working a full day to properly install. Herb's new product, originally designed by his uncle, Morris Tyre of Los Angeles, was part of the revolution in rapid home construction during the early 1950s. His doors were prepared at the warehouse rather than on the job site; they were sized to fit the door jamb and had the hinges already in place. "Pre-hung" doors could be installed in an hour or so by even the unskilled handyman or homeowner.

The name of our new business was the Allied Building Supply Company, and our warehouse was located in the depressed industrial section of East Oakland. I'll never forget those first few weeks of "basic training" in the door business. In an office barely large enough for the two desks,

Herb's and mine, and the telephone that we answered with the names of both companies, "Broadway Glass" and "Allied Building Supply," we contacted building contractors, took orders, mailed invoices, designed stationery logos, and shouted to be heard over the constant roar of the buzz saws in our adjacent workshop. Every surface was piled with blueprints, plans, orders, and scribbled memos, and on top of everything was a layer of fine sawdust. Mr. and Mrs. Lipkin ran Broadway Glass from an outer office. It was constant pandemonium. Herb never sat still: standing, sitting, gesturing, shouting into the phone, calling orders to the men in the shop. In the midst of this frenzied activity he taught me the business. I learned about door jambs and casings, contracts and building permits, invoice and office procedures. At the end of my "basic training" Herb handed me a long list of leads: contractors, builders, owners, and suppliers, and said, "Knock 'em dead, kid." I was on my own. It was like a story out of the movies. Every sale was critical and every unexpected bill a crisis. We worked eighty-hour weeks and drove hundreds of miles for a large order. Herb eventually bought me a company car, a used Plymouth, although I didn't have the nerve to admit that I didn't have a license. We ate on the run and I often slept on the couch at his parents' house. They took me in like family and I even learned a smattering of Yiddish around the dinner table. (How many former Afrika Korps veterans can make such a claim?)

IT IS IRONIC, considering that I grew up in Hitler's Germany and fought in the *Wehrmacht,* that one of my closest and most influential friends should be Jewish. In many ways it is puzzling to me as well, not because I overcame the virulent anti-Semitism of my youth, but because the anti-Semitism admittedly permeating German society did not find root in me from the beginning.

Anti-Semitism is such a peculiar historical malady. Since medieval times the Jews have been singled out as scapegoats for every imaginable ill. It was the early Christians who first planted the seed. They wanted to interest wealthy Romans in their new religion but could not very well succeed by blaming Christ's crucifixion on Rome. Only two other groups were available in Palestine: the Arabs and the Jews. They chose the Jews. By the Middle Ages it was fashionable to blame the Jews for anything from the Black Plague to lost wars. Medieval artists depicted Jesus as blond and blue-eyed to distance him as much as possible from his Jewish heritage.

Legislation restricted the Jews ability to own property and forced them into the most demeaning trades. Then they could be pointed out, discriminated against, and persecuted as the need arose. Martin Luther railed against the Jews, as did Karl Marx. France accused them of selling military secrets to the Germans, and the Russians blamed them for losing the Russo-Japanese War in 1904. If the Jews were poor they were despised for living off society; if rich they were hated for exploiting the masses. Given the traditional European acceptance of the Jews as popular scapegoats, Hitler had no trouble convincing Germany that they were responsible for our loss in World War I.

I was thirteen when the Nazis took over. While Schweidnitz was far off the beaten track, it was no less vulnerable to Hitler's promises of jobs and a resurrection of national honor. My brother, Paul, had been unemployed for ten years and most people in town agreed that the Weimar Republic that had signed the peace agreement in 1919 was largely ineffectual. That the Republic had a number of prominent Jews among its leaders only made Hitler's task easier. The Jews were depicted as powerful international bankers and cunning politicians, and I suppose, looking back, most of us probably agreed. But then we just didn't know many Jews. In fact, I remember only one Jewish business in town, a butcher shop near the Rathaus that I never paid any particular attention to. I vaguely recall passing their shop one day and noticing that they were no longer in business. When the headlines of our local paper, *Rundschau,* announced the exodus of Jews from Germany, I don't think we were surprised or particularly upset. I remember that there was a small synagogue in Schweidnitz and that it was just a boarded-up building with some broken windows; I passed it on my way to the soccer field. I realize how curious it must seem not to have noticed these things, especially since we now know how horribly it ended, but the Jews were just a distant abstraction to me. That attitude seemed to me to be shared by the powerful Protestant and Catholic Churches in Germany. As a frequent churchgoer, I recall no serious remonstrances to the congregation from the pulpit of the Gothic Catholic cathedral I attended and where I received my communion. Neither did the clergy, even in self-interest, seem concerned that what was happening to the Jews might foreshadow repression of the churches.

Now the appeal of the marching bands and cheering crowds is another story. Like all teenagers, I loved the martial music, the shiny boots and helmets, and the columns of heroic-looking men marching in cadence. I knew the words to their songs and dreamed about leading my men into battle against Germany's foes. Like most of my classmates I stood on the sidewalk and gawked at the brownshirt parades with their hundreds of swastika flags waving in the wind. I never wanted to be one of the soldiers, I remember, but I desperately yearned to be the strutting drum major at the head of the column. I would have given anything to have that shiny baton. But I somehow never saw the possibility of attaining that fantasy by joining the Party. When my friend Horst Trispel joined the Hitler Youth, I couldn't seem to afford the dues. At school I shrugged off the lecture I received from the principal about squandering my time in a "sissy" game like tennis instead of attending to my "political duties." When my biology professor occasionally appeared in his SS officer's uniform, my hatred of lizards and snakes overcame any appeal his outfit may have had. After I got sick with diphtheria, my dreams of becoming a drum major evaporated. When the illness left me with a temporarily paralyzed leg, I figured that they probably wouldn't want me anyway. I decided that I was better off trying to regain my health on the tennis court and the ski slopes. I just never got involved. My only experience as part of the swastika crowd came during my stint in the National Labor Service. A number of us were picked to march in the 1940 Nuremburg Party Day celebration, directly past Hitler's reviewing stand. I remember that we spent endless hours practicing the high-kick goose-step in columns ten men wide. However, nothing ever came of it. A few days before we were to leave for the rally we were told that the whole event had been canceled due to the invasion of France. I was miffed but hardly crushed. By the time I was discharged in September and returned to Schweidnitz to await my induction into the Heavy Artillery, the town was nearly empty. The Nazis had somehow passed me by. I was never particularly attracted by their promises or their racial myths. Consequently my first real contact with a Jewish person was Herb Lipkin, and I grew to like him a lot before it dawned on me that he was one of the "international bankers" whom I'd been taught to hate.

HERB AND I became close pals. We played tennis together on weekends and went skiing when we found the time. Several times a year we would pile into Herb's big Buick and drive up to Lake Tahoe, where he loved to gamble, and if we made a spectacular sale, he would drive us a thousand miles to Alta, Utah for skiing. Herb introduced me to my first steak dinner and martini at Art's Restaurant in Oakland and taught me how to meet new people of all types. I met his friends at the University of California in Berkeley who, in turn, introduced me to a wide circle of their own friends. Perhaps the most important thing I learned from Herb Lipkin was the ability to think on my feet: to make split-second decisions, rapid-fire calculations, and changes in my sales pitch. He was a bundle of energy whose enthusiasm was infectious. In almost every way, Herb changed my life. He gave me a respectable job, a business education, friendship, and trust. While I continued to teach skiing every winter, the rest of the year was spent selling pre-hung doors for Herb—every year until 1957 when he suffered a fatal heart attack at the age of thirty-four. That day I lost my best friend.

In 1951, however, we seemed to have it made. It was an exciting life. Allied Building Supply was poised between wealth and bankruptcy, and if I worked hard and got lucky, Herb and I would become the "pre-hung door kings" of America. There was also the prospect that my aluminum "Dennis Racquet" or other invention might catch on. I had a good job, friends, a car, and a future. I believed that I was finally safe in America. When I waved good-bye to the Lipkins in December to return to the Sierra Club for the season, I couldn't have imagined that anything could go wrong. How could I have known that I would be involved in the rescue of several hundred people, which would test the limits of my physical endurance and thrust my picture across the front pages of America?

THE SIERRA CLUB had not changed since the last season. All my "winter friends" were there as was my job as head ski instructor. The old Packard was up on blocks, though it was doubtful if it had another season left in it. I was even welcomed back by a big floppy hound that had "adopted" me the year before, a God-knows-what breed that Carla Wolff named "Menace" (as in "Dennis the Menace"). It was already shaping up into a record year for snow, and the lodges throughout the Sierra Nevadas were filled with skiers. It looked like a perfect season.

With the beginning of the new year, 1952, it started to snow more heavily. Snow is hardly unusual for that time of year in the mountains; that's what skiers pray for. But good cheer slowly changed to consternation as the snow continued day after day. By the middle of January, problems were starting to arise. Transportation between the various lodges, common in the past for both guests and staff members, was becoming quite difficult. Only the most adventurous people, driven by party plans or attracted by the lure of special ski runs, ventured out in tractor-drawn sleds. The Sierra Club, like the others in the area, was beginning to stockpile food and liquor for their snowbound guests. The snow continued for twenty-four straight days and nights, burying most of the buildings and isolating us from the rest of the world. We lived under thirty feet of snow and walked through a fifty-foot long snow tunnel, complete with electric lights and a bulletin board for messages and weather updates, in order to get from the main lodge to the adjacent dormitory and restaurant complex. It was all great fun in a terrifying sort of way. We were trapped but safe, although individual stories of fear, frolic, or heroism made the rounds of the ski community for years to follow.

Suddenly one afternoon the fun stopped. The westbound Southern Pacific streamliner, *The City of San Francisco,* had stalled in the infamous Emigrant Gap, trapping several hundred terrified passengers without food or heat. It was near the very spot where, in 1846, a wagon train of 81 California-bound emigrants led by George Donner was trapped for four months, the survivors cannibalizing the bodies of their 36 dead. This time, the diesel-powered wagon train carried 196 passengers and a crew of 30, and was trapped under 20-foot drifts a dozen miles from the nearest possible help. They only had food for one day and their diesel fuel would run out even sooner, plunging them into bitter cold darkness. Every bit of snow equipment in the Norden area was mobilized to forge a road to the trapped passengers, but that would take several more days. It was critical that a ski patrol somehow get through to them with the emergency food and medicine to survive until the massive rescue effort reached them. The Southern Pacific sent out a call for volunteers (the last time I answered a call to volunteer I ended up in North Africa and a prison camp), and as the head instructor at Sierra and a cross-country ski expert to boot, I stepped forward to lead the patrol. There was also a certain irony in helping the Southern Pacific Railroad, since they were the ones who made possible my escape from Camp Deming back in 1945 without a ticket.

Time was already running out for the 226 people on the train. They had been freezing in the dark, trapped beneath an avalanche of 20 feet of snow for three days before volunteers were called and our 11-man ski patrol set out for Donner Pass. Loaded with packs of food and medical supplies, our patrol plowed endlessly through the high drifts, stopping only to drink the hot soup in our thermos bottles. We knew that we were not only fighting the elements but time as well. If we didn't get to the trapped passengers

108

quickly, they would surely freeze to death. Hour after hour we struggled single file along the mountainsides and through passable ravines. It took us a full day to cover the 17 miles to the train. In the late afternoon we finally saw a glimpse of the train buried under a vast mound of snow. There were no lights from within since their fuel had long ago run out, and we approached with grave foreboding. To our joy the passengers were alive and apparently well, and they stumbled unsteadily down the aisles in disbelief at our appearance. We could see that they had been through a difficult time. The train cars were tilted away from the side of the mountain, and the passengers were huddled together in little groups wrapped in bedsheets, blankets, and even the upholstery material torn from the seats. Everyone seemed to be coughing continuously because of the moisture dripping down the inside of the steel cars and the stench of diesel fumes, which permeated the whole place. We distributed our food and medical supplies to the grateful people. I had brought a camera with me and took some pictures while we listened to some of their stories. When the fuel first ran out, the passengers burned the wooden Pullman ladders and kitchen breadboards for heat. On the second night they tried to raise morale by throwing a huge party, complete with singing, poker games, and a $100 lottery. A group of Republican committeewomen on their way to a meeting in San Francisco took the opportunity to campaign up and down the aisles to their captive audience. The only physician on board, a Dr. Walter Roehll, performed heroically to treat those overcome by fumes and to control a passenger who went berserk from drug withdrawal.

When all our supplies were distributed, it was time to decide what to do for the night. Many of the others in the rescue team had left, while some elected to spend the night. The passengers implored me to stay but one look around the cramped, freezing cars convinced me it was time to leave. My claustrophobia was already near hysteria; I knew I had to get out of the closed train and into the open air. (One man, a cook, wanted to come with me despite the fact that he didn't have skis or snowshoes. Ignoring my warning, he stepped off the train and disappeared into the thirty-foot snowdrift surrounding the train. It took a chain of passengers to pull the poor fellow back into the train, where he was welcomed like a hero.) Just before I left, the passengers gave me about a hundred letters and telegram messages that they asked me to mail when I hit civilization. I stuffed them into the front pouch of my parka, waved goodbye to the cheering crowd of well-wishers, and stepped resolutely out into the night. I backtracked the train line until I saw a light in the distance. It turned out to be a small cabin, an outpost of Skyline Lodge, where a friendly couple insisted that I spend the night. Despite the fact that the walls and ceiling were buckling under the weight of the snow on their timber roof, I slept like a rock. The next morning I set off for the nearest large resort, Nyack Lodge, where I could report on the safety of the passengers to anxious relatives and friends, and mail the letters and telegrams to the many more waiting for news around the country.

When I finally arrived at Nyack Lodge, overlooking Highway 40, it was nearly deserted. My friend Hershel Jones, the owner, informed me that they had not had any mail service for weeks. If I wanted to send the letters I was carrying and provide the world with the first photographs of the train and its passengers, I had to push on. Over a hot bowl of potato soup, Hershel told me that I was welcome to wait at his Nyack Lodge since a rescue caravan of nearly one thousand men with rotary plows, weasels, trucks, and automobiles were forcing a path toward us enroute to the trapped train. Doubtless, the rescuers would be accompanied by news reporters and cameramen—the very people I didn't want to face. Under the guise of having to deliver the mail and the photographs, I thanked Hershel for his offer to remain in the warm lodge and pushed off again in the direction of Baxter, California, about twenty-four miles away.

There is a terrible loneliness in skiing so great a distance by oneself, but at the same time, it is the ultimate challenge to one's endurance. I followed Highway 40, which was marked by periodic telephone poles with their porcelain insulators barely visible above the snow. After six or eight miles I suddenly encountered the slow caravan clearing the road to the Nyack Lodge. I waved and shouted that I was on too important a mission to stop. They wished me luck and I continued my grueling push toward Baxter. My original concern had been to let the world know that everyone on board the trapped *City of San Francisco* was alive and relatively well. Actually, that's not quite true. My first reason for this return trek was to escape the crushing claustrophobia of the dark stifling train cars. Then it became the need to herald the good news to anxious friends and relatives. Upon learning that the massive rescue was moving swiftly toward Emigrant Gap, close to the Nyack Lodge and the trapped train, my central concern then became to avoid publicity, especially any photographs of myself. Now that I was safely away from the rescue team, however, my new goal was to herald the good news *and* sell the first photographs of the disaster to the

110

press. I had done everything possible to help until the main rescue effort arrived, including risking my life, and now it was time to think about the value of the undeveloped photographs in my camera. You can't become a millionaire unless you look for the opportunities. After a long arduous trek, I dragged into Baxter about four in the afternoon. I estimated that I had skied about twenty-four tough miles. I turned the mail and telegrams over to the Baxter postmaster and headed out to sell the pictures. Luckily I was able to hitch a ride to Auburn, some thirty miles away, where I sold some of the pictures to the *Auburn Journal* in exchange for a fast ride to Sacramento. There I sold another batch to the *Sacramento Union* and United Press International. And believe it or not, I sold my last and most dramatic pictures of the wrecked train, its passengers, and our ski rescue team to *Life Magazine!* Oh my God!! My face would be among some of those group shots! I couldn't believe my stupidity, but there it was. When the article appeared on January 28, 1952, I held my breath as I scanned the photographs. There I was, on the edge of a group shot, but thank Heaven, badly out of focus. I was not so lucky elsewhere: every local paper within a hundred miles of Norden (and that's a *bunch* of newspapers!) carried a large close-up of "Dennis Whiles" as the leader of the ski patrol and the one who brought out the first pictures of the disaster.

I returned to the Sierra Club expecting to be arrested. Surely someone had recognized my face. Instead, I was welcomed like a hero and learned that the rescue caravan had broken through to Emigrant Gap, four and a half miles west of the streamliner, and a road crew dug out Highway 40 to a point where the passengers could walk out. Miraculously, only four required hospitalization. Sadly, I also learned that my dog Menace had bravely followed our ski patrol and had died in the snowdrifts looking for me.

Still, life quickly returned to normal. Skiers enjoyed a record season, and business was brisk at Bill Klein's ski shops. I basked in the occasional pats on the back for my part in the rescue. I had made a few hundred dollars on the photographs and even had the satisfaction of knowing that I paid back Southern Pacific for helping me escape from Camp Deming seven years before. On the other hand, I was terrified for the entire season that someone had recognized my widely distributed picture and that the FBI would arrive any day to arrest me in front of my friends and students. I could hardly wait for the end of the season to return to the safety of selling pre-hung doors for Herb Lipkin. To be on the safe side, however, I decided

111

it was time to change my base of operations and made quiet arrangements to teach at a different ski lodge the following year. Too many people knew me here, and between Carla Wolff's training films and my photograph in the local papers, it was getting dangerous to remain. The next season I went to Dodge Ridge in a completely different ski area several hours south of Norden.

IT WAS A terrible conflict to be in. Less than ten years earlier, I had been in Hitler's Afrika Korps, and now I was a respected ski and tennis instructor with a wide circle of friends. My off-season job with Herb was going splendidly and if pre-hung doors didn't make me rich, perhaps my inventions might. I had a car, girlfriends, and a future. It is one of the saddest requirements of being a fugitive that just when you have everything you strive for, success and friends, that is the moment when it's time to leave. That very success brings with it the public visibility that might well bring the authorities to your door. Too much visibility attracts unwelcome curiosity and in 1952 I decided to change my friends and locations. Such decisions are the loneliest and most wrenching part of being a fugitive. But survival is the name of the game.

FIVE

A FTER SUCH A tumultuous winter season I was grateful to return to the safety of selling pre-hung doors for Herb Lipkin in Oakland. Business had gone well during the winter months since the moderate temperature of California made home construction an almost year-round activity. The Eisenhower years saw a boom in home construction due to a combination of general prosperity, the availability of the GI Bill, and a middle-class exodus to the developing suburbs. Oakland was already considered a "bedroom community" for San Franciscans who commuted to and from work, and even the sleepy farm and cherry orchard town of San Jose, fifty miles south, was engulfed by housing developments. Herb and I figured that everyone needed doors and that there was a fortune to be made. Success depended on our ability to cover as wide an area as possible if we hoped to connect with big orders. That meant long hours and plenty of driving. The hours didn't worry me but the constant driving certainly did. Perhaps a dozen times a week I found myself next to a police car, waiting for a red light to change or for a traffic jam to untangle. Those moments seemed like hours as I fought the impulse to look over and see if I was being stared at. I didn't want to arouse the least bit of curiosity. If I looked too sullen or aloof they might be irritated enough to take a closer look. On the other hand, if I seemed too chummy that might also raise their suspicions. Clearly, I would not be able to withstand even the most cursory inquiries. I didn't have a driver's license or, for that matter, any identification that would satisfy a routine pull-over. It was several years before I got tired of thinking up excuses for Herb's insurance forms and risked applying for a license in the name of "Dennis Whiles." When I finally did, to my surprise and great relief, my California driver's license routinely appeared in my mailbox. (Even now, thirty years later, I am still very apprehensive about a close look at my license and developed the devious habit of carrying a saucy picture of my wife in a bikini just opposite the license, to distract the cop's interest.) In the early 1950s, however, the prospect of a routine encounter with the police made every day on the road a frightening experience. But anxious or not, the keys to success in sales are volume and contacts, and those require constant movement. My route might easily take me as far south along the East Bay as Hayward or even the entire fifty miles to San Jose, then across the Dumbarton Bridge, and up the peninsula side of the Bay through Sunnyvale, Redwood City, San Carlos, Palo Alto, San Mateo, San Francisco, and then back across the Bay Bridge to Oakland. It was a wide sweep, and often lucrative, but fraught with danger for someone who couldn't stand up to the most routine traffic inquiry. Over the five years that I worked for Herb, I must have put 100,000 miles on that old green Plymouth.

ONE OF THE places that I began frequenting more and more often was the university campus area in Berkeley. Herb and I occasionally played a few matches on weekends at the Berkeley Tennis Club, the spawning ground for some of the world's great players: Don Budge, for example, who beat Gottfried von Cramm of Germany in one of the classic 5-set matches of all time. More recently, the Berkeley courts produced such national champions as Bill Hoogs and Jim McManus, to name but two. When Herb and I first began playing there, the reigning champion was Frank Kovacs, ranked third in the world. Frank was a huge man, 6'6", and handsome as a movie star; he was related to a movie star, in fact, the comedian Ernie Kovacs. Herb often left me at the club when he had to visit a local client or girlfriend, so I began to make friends with other players. Frank and I played regularly and through him I soon had a wide assortment of acquaintances. A number of us developed into a tight circle of friends who were to last for many years, several even to this day. Eventually, I moved out of my place in Oakland, near Herb on 33rd Avenue, and found a nice little rooming house, owned by a wonderful woman named Mrs. Hungerford, on the outskirts of Berkeley. While I always went to the slopes in winter, I returned like a homing pigeon to my attic room at Mrs. Hungerford's on Montecito Avenue every year until 1959.

What I liked best about my new crowd was that they were all unique. Everyone was different enough so that I wasn't worried about standing out. It was amazing to think that despite my noticeable German accent, my quirk about looking over my shoulder, and the fact that I didn't have a past—I was still the most average person in our group. Our traditional hangout after playing tennis was LaVal's Pizza Parlor on Shattuck. Most Saturday afternoons were spent around our large table where we were joined by a regular crowd, including a history professor and several grad students. The pitchers of beer would arrive and we'd settle in for an hour or two of heated debate on any subject. It was a lot of democracy for me to handle, but I eagerly looked forward to each "seminar." Even quiet, these fellows were interesting.

First, there was Lowell Welch. Blond, crew cut, blue-eyed, and immaculately dressed, Lowell looked like a U-boat commander. Early in our friendship, which was to last twenty years, I actually had to resist the urge to click my heels when he asked me a question. Lowell was married to Yvonne. They had two children and lived on a substantial family inheritance. He talked about working only when he hit upon a gimmick like a fast real estate deal or the financial possibilities of my aluminum tennis racquet. Aside from tennis and get-rich-quick schemes, Lowell loved to dance. To my delight, he often invited me to go with him and we spent many evenings at places like the Rose Room where, for 10 cents a dance, you could take a spin around the floor with one of their smartly dressed and cheerful ladies. It was a perfect way for me to meet girls, since I didn't have Lowell's blond good looks, and I knew that the relationship would not have to last any longer than the number of 10-cent tickets in my pocket. If my dance partner asked too many probing questions about my past or accent I had the option of picking out a new partner. Lowell was a great friend who continued to pop in and out of my life long after I left the Berkeley area in 1959. We were surprised several times to find that we had moved to the same communities, which was not only a lot of fun, but his friendship "legitimized" me in each new community. Here, after all, was someone who could vouch for my unknown past, a dyed-in-the-wool American who put to rest any suspicions about me by employers, neighbors, or my own wife. It was reassuring to be able to introduce Lowell to new friends as someone who knew me "in the old days." As an expert tennis instructor himself, he also gave me the credibility to get established as an instructor and tournament player.

Then there was Sidad Serman, to whom Lowell introduced me on the Berkeley courts. Short and swarthy with a smooth shock of black hair, Sidad or "Sid" as we all called him, was a foreign student from Turkey. Like all of us, he was a good tennis player, but his real passion was women and the conspiracies required to maintain half-a-dozen relationships simultaneously. He was clearly glad to be free of the rigid social restrictions of his Muslim homeland and relished the limitless opportunities of the Berkeley campus. Sid's antennae were always alert for a passing possibility, and he was evidently quite successful. Whenever he missed a serve on the tennis court or ran out of steam midway through a tough doubles match, he blamed it on sexual exhaustion. Like Romeo back at Clinton's and Tim at Sugar Bowl, Sid was willing to share his vast knowledge, and we were certainly eager to learn. At the end of a typical description, which usually involved several lusty girls and gymnastics that made us pant, he imparted a kernel of wisdom, some sage advice to guide us through our pathetic lives. "Keep them off-balance," he told us, as we nodded understandingly. "And never, never let one girl find out about the existence of another."

I once violated this last ironclad rule when I turned to one of Sid's dates during a Saturday afternoon get-together and asked about a girl that Sid had brought the week before. I was under the impression that they knew each other, or at least knew about each other. Was I wrong! The girl ground her teeth and Sid fired a look across the table that could have melted steel. He later gave me a dressing down the likes of which I haven't had since basic training in the German Army. "If you want to make it in the real world, Dennis, you have to learn to keep a secret!" he bellowed. "You have to learn to keep parts of your life separate from each other, and for heaven's sake, Dennis, think before you talk!" I was remorseful, of course, and apologized profusely for having created a problem for him. After pausing a moment to let the lesson sink in, Sid broke into a good-natured smile and we shook hands. Inwardly I was relieved that my oversight had not damaged our friendship, and promised myself to be more careful in the future. At the same time, I couldn't help laughing at the irony. Sid was telling *me* about the importance of keeping a secret. I had spent the majority of my adult life doing exactly that. Secrets!? Sid had no idea what kind of secrets I really had! I did learn a lesson, however: think before I talk! I realized that I was getting too comfortable and was forgetting about my safety. I was grateful to Sid for unknowingly clearing my head and reminding me to be more careful.

Moving around the pizza table one came to Lionel Wilson. Lionel had just finished law school and was preparing to enter politics. He was married to a beautiful redhead named Dorothy, and they had two kids. When I first met him on the courts, he was running for alderman with an ambition for higher office. In fact, Lionel won and became the first black alderman in Berkeley. He went on to become the mayor of Oakland—not once, but for three consecutive terms. (Another member of our table, George Dufort, rose to become an assistant district attorney, and, incidentally, stood up for me at my wedding to Jean in 1964. Only in America.) I last saw Lionel in 1972 when we found ourselves playing at the same celebrity tournament in Pebble Beach. I recall that we reminisced on life's good fortune and considered ourselves lucky to both be happily married and enjoying tennis at middle-age. To complete the table there was Ed Christien, a superb athlete, who was a senior telephone executive in San Francisco.

Outsiders were welcome, but few survived many weeks of our boisterous arguments on subjects ranging from the philosophy of ancient Greece to modern history and art. Our discussions were always stimulating and often focused on issues of the day. We spent one entire afternoon discussing foreign policy, another on the reasons for the skyrocketing divorce rate, and yet another on the oft-debated question of whom you would allow in the limited space of your home bomb shelter. On one very uncomfortable afternoon we discussed the horrors of the Holocaust in Nazi Germany. You can imagine how I squirmed that afternoon. Though I left my German past far behind me and have always been horrified at the Nazis' genocide of the Jews, I remained silent throughout the whole discussion. I was afraid that if I became excited I might say the wrong thing or perhaps speak in German. What if I inadvertently corrected the pronunciation of a general's name or showed too much knowledge about military or political matters? All eyes would surely have been on me and then the questions would have begun. I had plenty to say on the topic of Nazi Germany but I decided to lean back and silently follow the debate. Sid asked my opinion several times but I just shrugged and admitted my ignorance on the subject. I wish I could have reminded him about his recent lecture to me about the importance of keeping a secret.

WHEN I WASN'T on the courts or in LaVal's Pizza, I was driving endless hours to sell pre-hung doors to the contractors of Northern California. I suppose that it was only a matter of time before I had an accident, with all the horrors that represented. The only actual driving experience I had before I went to work for Herb, aside from a two-week course as a teenager on the empty narrow roads of Schweidnitz, was an occasional stint behind the wheel as a migrant worker in the San Joaquin Valley. Those few times behind the wheel were hardly sufficient preparation for the constant surprises on the packed streets of Berkeley with students darting about on bicycles and cars turning sharply to avoid obstacles and pedestrians. To complicate matters, Herb's old green Plymouth had a standard stick shift, which may be great on the highway but was a real pain in the traffic of a busy university town.

One day it happened. I was threading my way down a side street choked with double-parked cars and kids darting across from every angle, when a car suddenly pulled out from the curb. I slammed on the brakes but it was too late. The front of his car bashed into the passenger side of my old Plymouth. We both got out of our cars to inspect the damage, which was relatively minor. He was a harried Berkeley student who apologized profusely, his words tumbling out as he successively told me that he had been thinking about his exams, that the car belonged to his father who would beat him to a pulp, and that he had never had an accident before today. People were beginning to gather on the sidewalk to survey the damage and discuss responsibility for the accident. I was already shaken by the bash from his car and was growing terrified at the prospects of what might follow. Somebody had called a traffic cop. There would be questions and an exchange of drivers' licenses. All I could think of was some way to leave before the police arrived. I'm sure the kid couldn't imagine why I was so nervous as we stood around kicking the tires and picking at the dent. Suddenly I couldn't take the tension any longer. I told the startled kid that I had been on my way to a big business deal when we collided and that I had to go after it. My company was depending on me, I told him, and so was my family. Actually, I didn't give him much choice. I pulled out my business card, pressed it into his hand, and got back in my car. Even though the business card was real, I figured anything was better than waiting around for the police to arrive. I'd worry about the repercussions later. First I had to get away from there.

Herb took it all surprisingly well. "O.K., so those things happen," he shrugged. "We've got insurance, after all, so why worry? Besides, it wasn't even your fault; the other driver had clearly been in the wrong. Why don't we just wait and see what happens?" Herb was wonderful about it, and I was greatly relieved. He could have shouted or taken the car away from me or, for that matter, fired me. Besides, what was a dented car to the future pre-hung door kings of California? Herb told me to stick close to the shop for a couple of weeks until the driver or his insurance company contacted us. That was fine with me. I was still a little gun-shy about getting back in the car. Too many things could go wrong. Maybe I was becoming accident-prone, or my driving was simply too poor. Moreover, a dented car might attract the interest of a passing cop. I decided that Herb was absolutely correct and that I should work in the office for a while. I could use the rest and had a number of projects I could do.

The first was to design a logo for our company. Since I had some artistic ability, Herb suggested that I put my "vacation" to good use. The result was a smiling little man balancing a stack of doors on one hand and holding a "SALE" sign in the other. Not Picasso, I grant you, but eye-catching for those years. After a few days I really began to get back into my art. I had always enjoyed painting and had studied to be an architect back in Schweidnitz. Art was a language I could communicate in without fear of making a mistake or raising suspicions. It was fun to impress people with a hidden talent, especially girls with whom I was still terribly shy. Painting also allowed me to meditate in peace, a kind of retreat from the bustle of the world. I often doodled to pass time and daydreamed about one-man exhibitions, gallery shows, and a large public following. I had already sold my first painting, after all, to the American guard at Camp Deming when I set up an easel at the fence-line to time the schedule of the distant train. Maybe if I worked at it during my spare time I could sell a few paintings and create an extra income.

One day I read an announcement in the paper that there would be a sidewalk art show that anyone could enter for a dollar. I rented three upright panels, which formed a small booth. The show stretched the entire block along University Avenue in front of the campus gate. I hung up my best watercolors and settled into a chair to take in the sunshine and the strolling sightseers. Friday and most of Saturday passed as I sat answering questions about my style or "school" and basked in the role of the artist. Several people even bought paintings—genuine "Dennis Whiles"—for a few dollars. I was having a great time and was determined to do this again. When I came back from a break late Saturday afternoon I found an official-looking business card pinned to my booth. Squinting at the card I read the heartstopping words: "Mary D. Trumbul, State of California, Parole Board." Underneath, in bold handwriting, a message said: "Please see me at 211 Dwight Way, Suite #304." They'd caught me! I didn't know how they had found me but it was clearly over. I was grateful that the FBI preferred to have me surrender voluntarily rather than suffer the embarrassment of being arrested in the middle of the art show. I slumped heavily into my chair to weigh the options. My first thought, of course, was to disappear. I would miss Herb and my Berkeley friends and my dreams of becoming the king of pre-hung doors, but survival came first. But what if I was wrong? I decided to chance it and face the danger head-on. Overcoming the urge to postpone the confrontation for a few hours (or years), I marched like a condemned man to 211 Dwight Way. To my surprise I found myself facing a three-story red brick building with an ornate glass front door and a brass push-button panel. I rang 304 and was "clicked in." At the top of three flights of carpeted stairs I was met by a matronly looking lady. "Yes?" she asked with an uncertain smile. With deep misgivings I showed her the card. "Oh yes," she said. "You're the artist who painted that wonderful picture of Chinatown. How much do you want for it?" I almost fell off the couch. All she wanted was the picture!! I was so relieved I almost gave her the damn painting, but all I could force out was a mumbled "Would five dollars be O.K.?" She broke into a handsome smile and reached for her checkbook. When I reached the street, I almost jumped for joy. I felt reborn and resolved to keep my paranoia under better control—knowing at the same time that it was my paranoia that had probably allowed me to remain free as long as I had. I also conceded that however terrifying, a periodic shock was a healthy reminder to keep my wits about me and stay cautious.

IF I NEEDED a reminder about a perilous position, it came with a bang one day in May 1953. I was reading *Collier*'s Magazine during a lunch break at an outdoor restaurant, when I turned to an article entitled, "It's Easy to Bluff Americans." It was written by a German prisoner of war, a Reinhold

Pabel, who had escaped from a branch camp at Washington, Illinois, near Peoria, on September 9, 1945. I was astonished to read what sounded like my own story. Armed with only $15, which he had collected from loose change in the camp laundry, Pabel had slipped out of the camp and had hitchhiked some fifteen miles to Peoria. From there he caught a train to Chicago where, as "Phillip Brick," he worked as a pin-boy, dishwasher, shipping clerk, and a circulation worker on the *Chicago Tribune*. After two years of work, he had saved enough money to open a tiny bookstore on Chicago's near-north side, and a year later had done well enough to move to yet a bigger bookstore. Eventually the prospering "Dutch refugee" married an American girl, and their first child was born in June 1952. Apparently, he had almost forgotten that he was a hunted fugitive and even had the secretive pleasure of selling some books to a man he recognized as his former guard at the POW camps. Pabel's luck ran out on March 9, 1953, when eight FBI agents walked into his bookstore and arrested him. He was currently facing deportation.

I was in a state of shock. First, I hadn't really considered that there were other fugitive POWs on the loose. I knew that statistically there must have been others, but I never really thought about it. I always figured that I had been the only one. Now I learned that there were a total of six of us still being hunted by the FBI, and with the capture of Reinhold Pabel, the number dropped to five. I was one of only five successful escaped German prisoners in America! It was both terrifying and exhilarating. I was a member of an exclusive club and yet there were enough "members" to keep the FBI occupied elsewhere. For the first time I felt as though there were at least five other people in America who understood what I was going through. Men who looked over their shoulders, who changed names and jobs regularly, who abandoned their friends, and who experienced the same terror every time someone stared at them with undue interest. Like me, they had probably applied for Social Security cards and drivers' licenses and had developed their hobbies and previous skills into means of steady employment. They too had been tongue-tied in new social situations and confounded by strange idioms and phrases. Each had somehow learned to survive in a new country. I was amazed by the enormity of this new insight, and felt a strange bond with each man whose picture stared back from the pages of Pabel's article. I looked carefully at each mug shot for a sign of recognition: might he have been in my unit in the Afrika Korps? Maybe we bumped into each other in basic training or at officers' candidate school. Was there anything about them that made them stand out from the average American, something that might single me out as well? I searched each face for a familiar sign without success.

Harry Girth had been a twenty-year-old German paratrooper who escaped from Fort Dix, New Jersey, in June 1946, just two days before he was to be repatriated to Europe. Moving across the page I stared next at a picture of Kurt Richard Westphal, a burly former truck driver and merchant seaman who had escaped from Camp Bastrop, Louisiana, in August 1945. Next to him was a picture of Werner Paul Lueck, an escapee from Las Cruces, New Mexico, in November 1945. I turned to the last two pictures. Kurt Rossmeisl was a former officer in Rommel's crack 10th Panzer Division who escaped from Camp Butner, North Carolina, by pushing a wheelbarrow past several guards during a wood-gathering detail on August 4, 1945. Finally I stared at the last picture in the row. Georg Gaertner. It was an eerie feeling to look at a younger me, taken ten years earlier when I was photographed and fingerprinted after capture in North Africa. How naive I once was and how eager for adventure! Could I have ever imagined, at the moment that the photograph was taken at the POW processing station in Oran, that just ten years later I would be sitting comfortably at an outdoor restaurant in Berkeley, employed by a wonderful Jewish businessman, with a circle of interesting and devoted friends? Looking at the old me on the pages of *Collier's* was curious in several other ways. I felt a strange detachment from the Georg Gaertner in the photograph. It was me, of course, but a different me. In a sense, I was looking at the caterpillar before my metamorphosis into my present butterfly. I had experienced so much in the last ten years in America: travel, friendship, moderate successes, close calls, and above all, the freedom I longed for all my life. The young face on the page had no idea what wonderful times awaited him. I noticed another difference. I had become an American. I felt and thought and spoke like someone born in the United States. In many ways, like most immigrants, I was more conscious of being an American. I paid my taxes religiously (under different names) and was careful not to break any law, although my efforts to walk the straight and narrow were motivated by the fear that even the smallest violation might lead to a wider investigation and arrest. In forty years I don't think I so much as failed to return a library book. I was a good American. The face on the page was different: he was German.

When I finished reading the article, I noticed that I was not as frightened as I might or perhaps should have been. I really did feel detached from the young German soldiers in the magazine. I was also buoyed up by the knowledge that there were others in my position. I wished that I could have talked to them, perhaps all of us sitting around the table at LaVal's Pizza Parlor. We could have shared our unique experiences and exchanged survival techniques. We might have recalled our days in the army, the tragic-funny stories that veterans of every war enjoy sharing with their comrades. Of one thing I was certain: we would not have spoken in German. We had worked too hard to purge our native language from our thoughts to chance its revival. In fact, I doubt if many of us even remembered enough German to carry on a lively conversation. In my case, a decade of conscious effort to forget German already created huge gaps in my vocabulary. Thirty years later, as I write these words, I doubt if I could read the menu in a German restaurant. But no matter. We would have a marvelous conversation anyway. The greatest relief of all would have been to share my fugitive secret with another human being. I never told a living soul, however close the friendship or how harmless the stranger. Nor would I for the next three decades, until now. How good it would have felt to unburden myself.

Whatever the outcome of the article, I knew the dice had been thrown. My picture was now on millions of newsstands, coffee tables, and in doctors' waiting rooms across the country. Short of trying to tear up every issue in America or growing a full beard, there was nothing I could do. I had to learn to live with it and hope that readers would see as great a difference between Georg and Dennis as I did. I made a mental note to remember the names of my fellow club members and to watch the papers for any mention of their capture. I planted their names in my mind: Girth, Westphal, Lueck, a Rossmeisl. I decided to periodically check their wanted posters at the post office; if a poster was removed it meant that our five-man club had lost a member.

On rare occasions I did, indeed, spot a news item about one of my fellow members but it was not until years later that I learned about their fates. Harry Girth, the paratrooper who had escaped from Fort Dix, New Jersey, made his way to Philadelphia where, like me, he found a job as a dishwasher. He changed his name to Henry Kolmar, saved enough money to move to Atlantic City, and developed his interest in painting and design to open his own interior design business. Like millions of legal immigrants to America, his hard work paid off and he prospered. Within a few years

Girth owned a $5,900 shore home, an apartment in New York, an automobile and, at the age of twenty-seven, made plans to marry an attractive divorcee with a ten-year-old son. Only weeks before the wedding, Reinhold Pabel's article appeared in *Collier's* Magazine and his future mother-in-law recognized his photograph and convinced him to surrender to the authorities. I could not have known it at the time, of course, but even as I was reading the magazine on that sunny day in May 1953, the first member of my new-found club was surrendering to the New York Police Department. Girth quickly married his fiancee, which, after a period of voluntary exile in Mexico, enabled him to return to the United States and apply for American citizenship. Now there were only four of us.

Werner Paul Lueck, the escapee from Las Cruces, New Mexico, was located in Mexico City on July 27, 1954, interrogated by the authorities, and released. There were only three of us left.

Kurt Rossmeisl, from Rommel's 10th Panzers, escaped from Camp Butner, North Carolina, and caught a train that took him to Chicago. For the next fourteen years, Rossmeisl lived under the name of Frank Ellis and worked as punchpress operator, bartender, and elevator operator. He melted into the work force and became a model citizen. Rossmeisl obtained a Social Security card, insurance policies, and even joined a Moose Lodge in Chicago. He later told the authorities that his closest call came with the appearance of the same *Collier's* article that led to Harry Girth's arrest. Several of his fellow workers at the factory teased him about resembling the photograph of the German fugitive, but he was able to laugh it off until it was safe to change jobs and friends. Six years later, on May 10, 1959, the 52-year-old Rossmeisl, lonely and suffering from arthritis, and evidently tired of looking over his shoulder, simply walked into the FBI field office in Cincinnati, Ohio, and surrendered to the startled agents. At an immigration hearing on June 4, Rossmeisl was ruled deportable but was permitted to leave the country voluntarily so that he might reenter as a regular immigrant and apply for American citizenship. Our club now contained only two members.

Kurt Richard Westphal, the merchant seaman who escaped from Camp Bastrop, Louisiana, had somehow successfully escaped to Europe under the name of Charly King. He was apprehended in Hamburg in 1964, interviewed by several local newspapers, and, for lack of legal precedent or public interest, was released.

With Westphal's capture in 1964, the exclusive club of fugitive prisoners of war dropped to one: me. In retrospect I am glad that I didn't know what was happening to my comrades for the thought that they were still out there often sustained me when I felt like throwing in the towel and walking into an FBI office. Had I known that since 1964 I was the only one left, I might easily have succumbed to my loneliness and given up. Somehow, I didn't want to disappoint my four unknown comrades.

Understandably, my FBI files for mid-1953 show a dramatic increase in "Georg Gaertner sightings" as the result of the *Collier's* article. I was spotted in cities ranging from Memphis, Tennessee, where the FBI closed in on a hapless suspect with a German accent, to Columbus, Ohio, where a poor door-to-door salesman for *Encyclopaedia Britannica* who evidently resembled my picture in *Collier's* was turned in by a vigilant housewife. Every sighting was thoroughly investigated but, as always, with "negative results." Results aside, my files indicate that the FBI had certainly not given up on catching me, which, in turn, makes me feel better about the excessive caution I lived with and the many friends I did not endanger.

COLLIER'S ARTICLE OR not, my life had to go on. Besides, things were going quite well. During the winter months I routinely went back to my job at Dodge Ridge Ski School, and as always had a wonderful season. I missed the excitement and professionalism of working for Bill Klein at Sugar Bowl and the interesting, wealthy people whom he attracted. Bill and I were still good friends despite my decision to go it on my own. He understood that I was anxious to become an independent instructor, especially when I found myself working for a small percentage of the fees I was being paid. It was perfectly normal that I should try to better myself. What he didn't know, of course, was my reason for moving to an entirely new ski area: the appearance of my photograph in every local paper following the train rescue made me too nervous to return. I reasoned that if the chances of my arrest were still only one in a hundred, why risk it? Besides, Dodge Ridge was a lovely place to work. My fellow instructors, Eric Johnson, Al Vokietaitis, Fred Spidell, Wayne Wiisanen, and Vaux Mervy, were great skiers and every arriving busload of resort guests brought the possibility of a new romance. I also had more self-confidence now and could talk with authority about other resorts and fine skiers I had known. I had proven myself during the train rescue and was accepted by all. Best of all, Dodge Ridge allowed me to work as a weekend instructor when Herb needed me in Oakland during busy periods. And business was booming.

Housing construction in the Bay Area was increasing dramatically and everybody in the building supply business was delighting over bigger and bigger accounts. For all our jokes, it seemed that Herb and I might well become rich after all. But the business boom also brought competitors and we soon found ourselves scrambling for our share. We grumbled at the injustice of it all. When no one in the area ever heard of a pre-hung door, we worked like crazy to show constructors the benefits of our products; now that business was booming, little companies were popping up like mushrooms and we had to work incredibly hard to stay afloat. Herb and I began to work long hours to cover an ever-widening sales territory. The problem of my traffic accident melted away anticlimatically when the other driver's insurance company contacted Herb for an estimate of the damage and routinely mailed him a check, so I was now back in my old green Plymouth. Herb covered a long route in his car and even Herb's father, old Herman, brimming with sound business advice, Talmudic wisdom, and lively humor, chased accounts in his battered station wagon. It was just like the old days: starve and gorge, starve and gorge. When we sold a big order Herb would take us all to Art's Restaurant for steaks, or he and I would get into the Buick and go skiing or find a tennis tournament. The majority of the time, however, we worried about bills and our competitors. To supplement my income over the next several years I worked weekends at Dodge Ridge, gave occasional tennis lessons, and even sold baby portraits door-to-door.

By 1956 and 1957 Allied Building Supply was decidedly in the black. The lean years appeared to be behind us. My friends were delighted with my success since I now picked up the check periodically at our Saturday afternoon "seminars" at LaVal's. We had been together for more than five years by now, perhaps the longest period I had kept the same circle of friends, and beamed at their successes as well. Lionel Wilson was already the first black alderman in Berkeley and on his way to being a judge; Frank Kovacs had gotten married; Lowell Welch was dabbling in real estate; Ed Christien had been promoted to dizzying heights in the telephone company and was currently driven to make me understand the game of football; and Sid ("The Turk") was still pursuing the ladies with the singlemindedness of a parched man in the desert. The crowning moment of change came when Herb announced that his new wife was expecting a baby and that he'd be spending a lot more time at home. I was elated to see him so happy though I admit to a tiny feeling of resentment in losing my tennis-skiing-business chum. On the other hand, it was a positive sign that the business was doing well enough for him to afford a family. Herb's marriage also started me thinking about the possibility of marrying someday myself. I was getting pretty tired of eating in fast-food drive-ins, taking my clothes to the Chinese laundry, and, frankly, being alone. I never learned any domestic skills and regretted that the Wehrmacht Officers' School in Heidelberg didn't show me anything more than how to boil water and wash fruit in strange lands. But, as always, I quickly dismissed such tantalizing daydreams when I realized the dangers of so awesome a step, both to myself and my unknowing future wife. Besides, bachelorhood wasn't so bad, especially now that Herb's business was rolling.

It was that very upswing in our business that led to a new problem and a parting of the ways with Herb and Allied Supply. In an effort to hold our hard-won niche in the market, Herb one day announced that he was hiring a new salesman, a high-powered veteran of the trade with one of the biggest contractor's accounts in his back pocket (and a fondness for the sauce that teetotaling Herb was willing to overlook). I felt sure that I was being eclipsed after so many years of loyal service and frankly my pride was bruised. When Herb further announced that he was taking me off salary and putting me on commission, the same as the new salesman, I decided it was time to change jobs. I understood Herb's position, of course; it was good business sense to hire someone who was bringing in an admittedly substantial account. He would have been foolish not to. My bruised pride aside, the new changes made my future a bit wobbly. Herb and I were close friends and I knew that he was not trying to get rid of me, but the prospect of being taken off salary and facing the future on the commissions from my sales was risky business. Things would be fine as long as the California construction boom lasted, but what if there was a downturn? How many weeks or months could I survive if I hit a sales slump? I discussed my concerns with Herb who reluctantly agreed to let me look for a new job. We parted good friends and continued to see each other regularly on the tennis courts and at LaVal's. Later that year, 1958, we learned that Herb had suffered a minor heart attack, the result, we agreed, of his dawn-to-dusk work habits. Shortly into the next year we were stunned to hear that Herb had succumbed to a fatal second attack. For most of us at the Saturday afternoon "seminar," it was the end of an era.

CHANGING JOBS HAD been a scary task for me. Thanks to Herb's training, I was now a seasoned millman-estimator, a recognized job in the California construction industry. There were dozens of building supply companies in the huge Bay Area and I hoped that I wouldn't have too much difficulty in finding a new job. My real fear was filling out those applications. "When and where were you born?" "What grades did you attend?" "What was your major?" "List the names of three references." For many evenings I sat in my little attic room on Montecito rehearsing answers to any imaginable application question or personal interview. I had to be prepared for anything that a foreman or supervisor might ask, like "What did your father do?" or "Were you in the service during the war?" I had to decide on every answer before I started making the rounds of supply companies. The biography I polished had been my standard life story since I applied for my Social Security card, even to my wife of twenty years. Dennis Whiles was born in New York City (lost in the statistics of tens of millions of others), his parents were both killed in a tragic automobile accident when he was a kid (which accounted for a total absence of relatives as well as an under-standable reluctance to discuss such a painful childhood trauma), and he received all of his schooling at a Catholic orphanage called the Connecticut School for Boys (since I knew nothing about the public school system, grades, or curriculum—was the 1st grade higher than the 8th?— I could safely invent any school program I wanted). On the matter of military service I ran into a problem. There was no way of knowing what branch of service my interviewer or foreman might have been in, where he might have been stationed, or what stories he could want to swap. If I listed the army or navy there was always a chance that he would ask my unit or other details. In the early days I had said I was 4-F, but I decided now that I had to put down some service. Ultimately I decided on the Merchant Marines—I have never yet met someone who was in the Merchant Marines. I even invented, for occasional use, a former wife who died in childbirth, in case I had to explain my continued bachelorhood at age thirty-eight or account for my shyness with women. Just the periodic reference to such a sad story caused people to overlook my occasional slip-ups or suspicious quirks. After all the details of my biography were worked out and well-rehearsed, I started making the rounds of building supply companies in the east Bay. One of the companies I called asked me to come in for an interview and, as miracles sometimes happen, the manager had heard of me through the trade and hired me without even filling out an application! "Fill it out when you start work on the first," he called over his shoulder as he strode out of his office enroute to another appointment, shouting orders to his secretaries as he left. I was now working for Emsco Plywood Company in San Mateo.

The real change in going to work for Emsco Plywood was not the job itself but the locale. It is hard to imagine a more dramatic difference in climate and living styles than the short difference from the East Bay area of Berkeley and Oakland to the Peninsula between the Bay and the Pacific Ocean. San Mateo, where I now lived, was just below San Francisco and shared the long winter months of rain and hazy mist, and was totally different from the rolling hills of Berkeley and Oakland where daily sunshine was the rule and three consecutive overcast days became a topic of conversation. The difference in climate produced an entirely different environment, from the flowers to the attitudes of the people. There were other changes as well. Unlike the generally blue-collar feeling of the Oakland area, the Peninsula was upwardly mobile with lots of expensive cars and high-priced home construction. If it took a little time to adjust to the new climate of the Peninsula, the affluence of the people who lived there was easy to like. It was the perfect place for a salesman in my business. I found a little efficiency apartment at 116 Elm Street, just off El Camino Real, the highway that links the major communities of Sunnyvale, Redwood City, San Carlos, Palo Alto, and San Mateo, just as it did when the Spanish missionaries first traveled the route from Los Angeles to San Francisco.

Business was as good as I had hoped, and often better. I was one of six estimators working for Emsco Plywood, real "go-getters" who were further fired up by a weekly pep talk from our dynamic manager. We crisscrossed the length of the Peninsula chasing construction accounts, and before long I was being courted by other supply companies in the area. After almost a year with Emsco I was hired by an outfit called the Clark Door Company in nearby San Carlos. I worked there for the next five years. It was a family-type company that reminded me of my years with Herb Lipkin: several of us chased accounts, Alice McIntire ran the office, and George Clark hovered over prestigious jobs like the building of a special kitchen for Bing Crosby's home in nearby Hillsborough. I was having fun and a bit of financial success.

Life was going very well. Aside from business, I was still experimenting with my aluminum tennis racquet and occasionally painted a few watercolors for a local shopping mall art show. (One of them won a blue ribbon.) On free weekends I bounded back to Berkeley for a few sets of tennis and an afternoon at LaVal's with my friends. During the winter months I made for the slopes as always and in 1960 even landed a job behind the scenes at the Winter Olympics at Squaw Valley. (That winter I dislocated my shoulder, to the delight of Sid the Turk who now found it easy to beat me on the tennis court for months to follow.) Things were terrific. Even my paranoia was down. Granted, my fear of arrest was always just below the surface but even that was ebbing as I grew more and more comfortable with my life in San Mateo.

A LOOK AT my FBI files for that period helps explain why I was feeling particularly safe.

The FBI was temporarily tapped out for leads. Even sightings had slowed to a trickle. In early 1959 the Bureau turned to what was surely its last resort. Washington ordered each metropolitan office in America to check the current telephone directories for any spelling of "Georg Gaertner"! The phone book!! Did J. Edgar Hoover really believe that a wanted fugitive would list his real name in the phone book? Are American crooks that dumb? I didn't dare utter my old name even in the shower, let alone list it in the public phone book! But, orders are orders and the next inch of FBI reports consists of dutiful summaries from each city. Baltimore reported looking through their local directories "with negative results," followed by the Denver office for all of Colorado and Wyoming. The Philadelphia office reported that it had checked fifty-three phone books covering the principal cities in its area. Then came the Detroit office, Mobile, Knoxville, Cincinnati, and so on. The Pittsburgh office rejoiced in locating both a "George Gaertner" and a "George Jaertner" and both were interviewed at length "with negative results." The Boston office checked their directories all the way back to 1945, and the Los Angeles office examined the local directories of enough towns to fill two pages of single-spaced columns. By 1960 the FBI offices had shifted their scrutiny to county telephone directories. Whatever their logic, I had reason to feel momentarily secure. The key word is "momentarily" because it would only take one new lead or accurate sighting to bring the full weight of the authorities back on track. In the meantime I felt safe; I was making money, and enjoying life. Yet there was something missing. I was growing older and lonelier. I was getting tired of running alone.

MY FORTIETH BIRTHDAY had come and gone in 1960, and with it the usual anxieties of approaching middle age. Where was I headed in life? What had I really accomplished thus far? Who was I? Such concerns are normal for anyone passing forty but I had the additional complications of being a fugitive. Perhaps I had lied so often that I didn't know who I was myself? Even an actor who plays the same role on stage night after night must experience moments when he has to stop and remember whether he is the actor or the character he's playing. I've often wondered if other fugitives experienced the same uncertainties, although I suspect that anyone who lives in disguise, whether it is a cowardly bully or a married man cheating on his wife, undergoes a similar confusion. I had already been a fugitive for fifteen years, and as often as I considered myself finally safe, little shocks every few weeks brought me up short and reminded me that danger was never far away. It might be an unexpected official-looking form or an unusually long stare from a policeman who pulled up to me at a red light. The danger might not even come from a stranger but from an old friend like Joe Chinchiolo who remembered me from my years as "Peter Peterson." Living in California there was always a possibility that I would run into any of the hundreds of people who knew me from earlier days: employers, tennis partners, old girlfriends, landladies, or migrant workers. Who knew who might come around any corner or call out my name in a crowded restaurant? It was a complicated way to live, however necessary, but I was getting weary of doing it alone. I longed for safety and companionship.

Companionship was available aplenty. There were bright, attractive, single people everywhere one turned, and I was never in a better social or financial position to attract them. But after I turned forty I began to wonder if I was not "over-ripe," and I started to look for girlfriends with different qualities. Subconsciously I was looking for a stable, long-term relationship though I thought that actual marriage was still too ominous to consider. I decided the best place to find a more serious relationship was at the singles dances that were held around the area. They were a long way from the 10 cent dances at the Rose Room where Lowell Welch and I went on Saturday nights. I really wanted to meet someone whom I could grow close to, not just to chat with until my tickets ran out. Girls of that era came to singles dances with hopes of finding a mate, and now that I look back on it, so did I. The first few dances were spent improving my social skills. I had to break away from my precise German foxtrot and learn some up-to-date dance steps. Next came the development of some interesting conversation chitchat, which I drew from listening to my friends at LaVal's. But the most interesting thing I learned at those early singles dances was that many men passed themselves off as bachelors when they were really married; it somehow gave me comfort to know that I was not the only person there who was masquerading as someone else.

It was at one of these singles dances that I met Barbara, and we embarked on what should have been a perfect relationship for me. Barbara was a lovely divorcée with dark hair and smiling brown eyes. She had a ten-year-old son from her previous marriage; that appealed to me as well. It was like having an instant family where I could be both "boyfriend" and "father." Barbara also loved sports, particularly golf, which I had never played, and she often took me out to the prestigious golf club where she worked as the club's executive secretary. Soon we were commiserating on the development of my "Dennis Racquet" and driving to golf and tennis tournaments all over the Peninsula. It should have been an ideal relationship: a mature career woman, with a young son, who was devoted to both sports and my success. As happens in the course of any ongoing relationship the subject of marriage cropped up, and I should have been elated to find that Barbara was the first to dismiss the idea. She was perfectly happy with the status quo and believed that marriage would only create new problems. She was a bachelor's dream, yet I took the news with a curious mixture of emancipation and dismay. At the time I didn't know why such news would bother me and attributed my mild depression to other aspects of the relationship. She didn't really like me, I convinced myself; perhaps she didn't think I would be a good influence on her son. Maybe I didn't make enough money to please her or my social skills were too unsophisticated. I soon talked myself into believing that Barbara was dissatisfied with our relationship and that no matter how hard I tried, she would never be satisfied. In retrospect, I now see clearly what had been bothering me—I longed for permanence and didn't know how to broach the subject—but at the time I could only conclude that Barbara and I were simply unsuited for each other. We went out less and less often and however painful the withdrawal, I steeled myself and returned to the world of singles dances, weekends on the slopes, and the daily chase for door accounts.

One evening in mid-May 1964, after a long stretch of overwork and general solitude, I shook off my laziness and went to a YMCA singles dance in nearby Palo Alto. Well into an uneventful evening, I suddenly spotted a tall redhead with an eye-popping figure and legs that didn't quit. I watched her dance from the sidelines and was almost too mesmerized to break in between songs. I remember bolstering my courage and walking up behind her to ask for the next dance. When she turned around, smiled, and said "Yes" I felt the fireworks that love songs are written about. Her name was Jean Bergmann. We danced the rest of the evening, my heart pounding like a high school kid, and by the time we stopped for coffee as I took her home, I was smitten. We talked until she started to yawn, and I could hardly wait to see her again.

Jean was a divorcée, I learned, and had two growing children: Mark, thirteen, and Lynn, sixteen "going on twenty." I was delighted that she had children, since I love kids, and was a bit surprised that she had been apprehensive about telling me about her brood at home. Over the next several months she told me about herself and I marveled at her independence and love of life. It was the kind of life I ached to share.

Jean Clarke came from northern California and grew up between Redding and Red Bluff. Her father worked for the telephone company and eventually retired as the manager of their Visalia facility. It was an austere household, a product of the depression years in California, and upon finishing high school in 1942, Jean said goodbye to her parents and her younger brother and sister, Willard and Beverly, and struck out to taste life. First came two years of college at San Jose State, but the excitement and patriotism of the war seemed to be passing her by. With a flair of independence, she quit school and joined the U.S. Cadet Nursing Corps. For the next two years she studied surgical nursing at San Francisco's St. Luke's Hospital during the day and spent her free evenings dancing with servicemen at the USO. On V-J Day, in September 1945, while I was staring through the barbed wire of a German prisoner of war camp in Deming, New Mexico, Jean was part of the exuberant parade down Market Street with a couple of joyous sailors on each arm.

In 1946 she married Harold Bergmann, an army musician home from the war. Marriage was every young lady's dream in those days; society said so. Lynn came along a year and a half later, and Mark in 1951. Society said she had fulfilled her role and should have been happy. But she wasn't. Her husband was a stable family man, but theirs was a stormy relationship. In 1947 Jean went to work for the California Department of Welfare as a social worker with the migratory farm laborers, and until Mark was born in 1951, visited the Hoovervilles and migrant camps up and down the San

133

Joaquin Valley. I listened to Jean's poignant descriptions of those camps and the problems of the migrant workers who followed the crops in wide-eyed silence, desperately wishing that I could tell her that I was one of them. I would have given anything to tell her that the moderately successful construction salesman who was sitting across from her at Nick's Restaurant overlooking the Pacific Ocean, who was trying hard to impress her with stories about tennis and skiing and painting, had been among the very people she was describing. How could I explain that I had taken my name from the migrant family I lived with? Who I was before? Why was a young man from New York, a graduate of the Connecticut School for Boys, working as a migrant laborer? No! I decided that I couldn't say anything yet. I didn't want to scare her off or have her turn me in to the police. She had been patriotic enough to quit school to join the U.S. Cadet Nursing Corps and had spent her evenings at the USO sending the boys off to war. I couldn't tell her yet. At the very least, such knowledge would legally make her an accomplice. I decided to say nothing, and once we got married, it was just too awkward to start. For the next twenty years Jean never knew who I really was.

She told me about living in Fresno with her family during the early 1950s, working as a YWCA program director and Red Cross Water Safety Instructor. In her spare time, she studied clinical psychology at Fresno State. Her marriage, however, was falling apart, and in 1958 Jean filed for divorce and moved with her kids to San Francisco. Life now became a daily struggle to keep her kids fed and the rent paid. Eventually she answered an insurance company ad for female recruits and was accepted for their management training program in New York. The kids went to her folks in Visalia while Jean learned a new profession. Three months later she returned and soon rose to become the first woman office manager-trainee of Mutual of New York Insurance Company's agency in San Francisco; by 1961 Jean headed the Berkeley branch; and by 1963 she had a fancy office in Palo Alto, the plum of the Bay Area. She was now a woman of substance. She was dating a man named Stan, although their relationship seemed to be deteriorating quickly. As a distraction to occupy her free time and because she loved to dance, she began to attend the monthly singles dances at the YMCA. To my everlasting gratitude, Jean decided to go dancing that night in mid-May 1964, and said "yes" to the anxious man who came up behind her on the dance floor.

We spent every Friday and Saturday evening together during that summer of 1964. When we weren't listening to each other's stories we were speculating about the future. On weekends we played tennis and golf and sat around the table with my friends at LaVal's. I worked hard to befriend her kids, having more luck with young Mark than with Lynn, who was defiant at my intrusion. In fact, Lynn dramatically announced that if her mother married me, she would kill herself! However serious her threat, Jean decided to continue our relationship in the hope that Lynn would grow to understand and moderate her hostility. Interestingly, it was Mark rather than Lynn who convinced Jean to continue seeing me. During the middle of the summer, Mark and his dad went on a fishing trip to Hungry Horse Dam in Montana. In the middle of the night, Jean got a telephone call telling her that young Mark had developed appendicitis and was undergoing surgery. Imagining her son in the hands of primitive Indian doctors, Jean flew to Montana in the middle of the night and brought him back, bent over with the stitches, on the Great Northern Railroad. When she arrived in San Francisco, frightened and broke, she had to decide whom to call—her old boyfriend Stan in San Francisco, or her new friend Dennis in San Mateo. She called me and I was at the terminal at breakneck speed. Running down the concourse in my Tyrolean hat, and taking them to a local hospital for postsurgical care, I so impressed Jean with my qualities of trust, obligation, and stability that she decided at that moment to stop seeing Stan and commit herself to our fast-progressing relationship.

From then on, it was a summer of candle-lit gourmet dinners and drives along the coast; of Sunday afternoons watching the kids swim in the pool at their Kendall Park apartment complex and the exchange of small gifts. By midsummer we were hesitantly talking about the possibility of marriage. Jean was exactly what I had been searching for in a partner. She loved life, adventure, and impish fun. People of all types fascinated her, and their suffering led her into a lifetime of social concern. At the same time, Jean took her professional life very seriously and always rose in the hierarchy to become office manager, supervisor, or director. She was liked and respected by her coworkers and often boasted that despite the instability in her private life, she had been unemployed only two weeks in her entire working life. Jean and her kids were everything I had always wanted. We decided to do it! After a short trip back to Visalia to inform her parents, we set the date for October.

Jean wanted to get married in a civil ceremony in Carson City, Nevada, and again at a church wedding at her favorite vacation spot, Zephyr Cove on the shores of beautiful Lake Tahoe. Since her elderly parents were unable to attend the weddings, and mine, of course, had been killed in a tragic auto accident in New York when I was a child, for witnesses we settled on Alice and Norman McIntire and on the most official personage we knew: my friend George Dufort, who had recently become the Assistant District Attorney for Placer County (which includes Lake Tahoe). An additional dozen assorted friends would drive up later for the reception and party that followed.

Our own drive up to Carson City for the ceremonies was the longest drive of my life. Driving to one's wedding is a period of deep introspection under the most normal circumstances. In my case I was panic-stricken. What questions would they ask me at the license bureau? "Are you an American citizen?" "Where is your proof of citizenship, please?" "Fill out these forms in triplicate, please." "Parents?" "Dates?" "Military Service?" I was getting wild-eyed as we got closer to Carson City. Maybe I should tell Jean the whole story right now? How would she react to learn that the man she was about to marry was really a former sergeant in Hitler's Afrika Korps and a wanted fugitive whose poster was on the wall of every post office and federal building? I decided that she would probably tell me to turn the car around and take her home. She had the right to know, but I didn't dare risk it. I kept thinking that I would tell her everything later on when we knew each other better.

At the same time I was understandably elated. I was going to get married! Me, the confirmed bachelor who was too shy to talk to women. Most men view marriage as an institution and lament the things they have to give up. What was I giving up? Loneliness? Cold food? I was starting a new adventure with a terrific woman who loved travel, sports, and art, and who had a keen business mind. Jean would be the closest and doubtless the longest friendship I had ever had before. Not only that, but I was going to have a family; kids whom I could teach things to and take care of. I knew I could be a good family man if I put my mind to it. If Horst Trispel from Schweidnitz could only see me now! I was about to become a legitimate American family man—unless I was arrested by the FBI during the ceremony.

I was shaking by the time we arrived at the Carson City courthouse. I was torn between the sweet joy of this new adventure and the terror of arrest or a lifetime of secrecy. Everyone attributed my rising panic to "wedding jitters," though my hand shook so hard while I was filling out the license that I dropped the pen. I made only one serious mistake, when asked if I had been married before. I had told Jean about a short, sad marriage to a schoolteacher earlier in my life, but when it came time to fill in the official forms, I looked at the question, "Have you been married before?" and, too rattled to think it out, answered, "No." I saw Jean's eyes widen with surprise and knew that I would have to come up with some answers when the smoke had cleared. I went through the next half an hour in a daze. I went where I was told, stood where I was told, and when I felt Jean jab me sharply in the ribs with her elbow, I blurted out: "I do." Thus began the sweetest and most painful part of my life.

SIX

I WAS A married man! Who would have believed it?! After the fiasco
at the Carson City courthouse and the calmer church wedding that
followed, we retreated to Harvey's Hotel on Lake Tahoe and became
children again. We laughed and played and ate wonderful meals and
whispered in the dark. I marveled at the wonder of it all. I had a wife!! I
finally had someone I could take care of, someone who would watch over
me. I also had two great kids waiting for me at their grandparents' in
Visalia, kids of my own! True, it was going to be a difficult task trying to
befriend Lynn, who deeply resented my intrusion into their little band, but
I figured that eventually she would come to realize that I was not taking her
mother away from her. I hoped it would be more like the situation where a
young child resents the appearance of a new baby brother or sister but soon
grows to accept and love it. Anyway, I reasoned, I had months or even
years to prove that I was not a threat to her established home life. I wonder
if I would have been as optimistic if I'd known how serious her resentment
really was and the number of troublesome times to come for her. Still, I was
determined to show her, and especially Jean, that I could be a good papa.

Jean was perfect for me. She knew that I had a number of quirks, but
never really pried. She didn't press me when I clammed up about my past
and graciously let me off the hook when I changed my story at the
courthouse about a previous marriage. I waited anxiously for her inevitable
questions but they never came. In fact, over the next two decades I'll bet I

could count the number of times on one hand that she bore down on a sensitive subject. Not that she wasn't curious, mind you; she just decided that it wasn't worth the strain and tension to our relationship that such questions always produced. She had just come from a difficult life, a divorcée with two youngsters, working hard to make ends meet. It would have been a natural reaction to trade curiosity for a safe harbor. Underneath it all, Jean is a California girl; the product of a culture that prides itself on tolerance and a pointed lack of interest in the past lives of others. She assumed that when I became evasive about my childhood or upbringing it was due to the terrible trauma of my parents' fatal auto crash and the difficult years of orphanage life that followed in the Connecticut School for Boys. I remained on my guard for years, wary of any unexpected turn in a conversation.

I don't mean to imply that my silence was any easier on me than on Jean. At the risk of sounding like a parent who is about to spank a child and says that "this will hurt me more than you," my evasiveness was probably more difficult for me than the suspense may have been for Jean. It was the old story: if I told her she might leave me in a huff, and if I didn't tell her, I had to learn to live with the anxiety of making a slip-up or of frustrating her with my silence. I always planned to tell her the whole story later down the road when we knew each other better. The fallacy, of course, was that we would never know each other any better since I was living behind a different identity. The giddiness and intimacy of our honeymoon weekend would have been the perfect opportunity to tell Jean who I was and how I had gotten here, but I chose to keep silent.

WHEN IT WAS time to return to the real world, we picked up the kids and began our life as a family in Palo Alto. I accepted the hearty congratulations of George Clark, Alice, and my friends in the construction trade, and the Dennis Whiles family settled into the middle-class routine. Our first priority was a big house of our own; no more Kendell Apartments living. After looking for some time we found our dream house: a new two-story wooden house at 845 La Para in Palo Alto. The owner let us move in with no money down so we could apply our limited funds to beautify the place to our satisfaction. I planted brilliant red bougainvillea against the white exterior and built a feminine room with a four-poster bed upstairs for Lynn, while Mark enjoyed a young man's room with carpeting and shelves for his precious model airplanes. It was wonderful to have a little family.

140

Jean and I were like kids, laughing and talking and cooking gourmet meals in the new pullman kitchen. For the first time in my postwar life I had a close friend, a friend I could talk to about *almost* anything. I had to adjust to the fact that I couldn't just leave Jean if things became difficult or if her questions about my past became too unsettling. I had to find a way to maintain intimacy without disappearing, as I had so often in the past. One solution was to be totally honest with my family from now on. I encouraged dinner-table discussions with Jean and the kids on every conceivable topic from art to politics. I now became a veritable chatterbox about the daily events in my life. I knew that I was overcompensating for the blanks in my early life, but I hoped that my new honesty would be sufficient compensation. A well-known artist in Chicago, Suzanne Cohan, once told me that truth is a powerful weapon. I was learning that she was correct, though I still could not bring myself to reveal the story of my early life.

Another interesting change brought about by married life was that I found myself relinquishing daily control. Jean enjoyed making the financial decisions, for which she has a decided flair, and I felt more and more comfortable placing such matters in her hands. She handled our leases and mortgage papers, signed the official forms, made our windfalls and reinvested it successfully. It was an easy habit to develop and, besides, I was tired of living on an emotional tightrope where every decision I made had to be cautiously examined for possible danger. In the past I had agonized over problems that were probably meaningless and others that might have been dangerous but became more dangerous by my endless worrying. Since Jean did not have any such concerns, it stood to reason that her decisions would be based only on the merits of the issue and not complicated by my convoluted rationalizing. Moreover, she had a clear head and the self-confidence of someone who has nothing to hide. Within a short time after we were married I gradually turned my problems over to Jean's capable hands and found that her suggestions about changing homes or trying new adventures were invariably correct and often exciting as well. There were times that she grew annoyed with the roles we had established and chided me for making her so responsible, but by those later years the pattern had become too comfortable to change.

While my marriage to Jean allowed me to become honest about current events and lifted the responsibility for decisions large and small, a number of old habits remained. For example, I always have a secret getaway fund. Even when we were down to the bottom of our bank account and getting worried about making a mortgage payment, I had a few bucks stashed away in case I had to bolt in a hurry. It was never more than fifty or seventy-five dollars, more like "mad money" as they used to say in the old days, but it was always there for a fast bus ticket or hotel room if danger suddenly appeared. Another habit I continued was to drive once around the block before going into the house when I came home. It didn't matter where we lived; I always circled the block looking for a suspicious parked car. Jean used to shake her head and the kids snickered at my unusual behavior, but they eventually just accepted it as a silly effort to find a better parking place. Finally, there was my lifelong habit of reviewing the days' events before I went to bed, examining every detail for a slip-up or potential problem. I called it my need to meditate on the problems of the day. These were my "survival routines," which didn't change from that day to this, whether we moved frequently or not. I reasoned that since Jean didn't know that I could be arrested at any time, I had to look out for my own safety.

One of the changes that I learned to enjoy was socializing. Jean loved to dance and mingle with her friends and became restless when we stayed home too often. Personally, I liked socializing, but I had always viewed such evenings as a means to an end, to meet girls, and had to train myself to enjoy dancing and party-going for its own sake. In a way it was part of the natural transition from bachelorhood to married life, enjoying an evening out *with* the person of your choice rather than to *find* the person of your choice. Jean made the transition fun, and we soon found ourselves partying up a storm. Jean had a circle of friends of her own, of course, and they accepted me with open arms. One of the closest friendships of those years was with Yvonne Baker, a blonde, middle-aged secretary at the Mutual of New York's agency where Jean worked as manager. Yvonne was married to a black businessman named Enos, and their frequent parties were well attended and lots of fun. Mixed marriages were rare in those days, even in California; in fact, Lionel Wilson, Oakland's three-term mayor, and his wife, Dorothy, were the only other mixed couple I knew. I've often wondered about my easy acceptance of people we were urged in Germany to despise, people like Herb Lipkin or Enos and Lionel, and can only attribute it to my embrace of America, and the fact that I "grew up" in California. In many instances I am more tolerant than the majority of native-born Americans I've met, but I attribute that to the "immigrant mentality." We foreigners are simply more conscious of the ideals, principles (and shortcomings) of the people we live among, if for no other reason than it helps us adapt with the least amount of friction or ridicule. In my case, I broke so completely with the first twenty-five years of my life in Weimar and Nazi Germany that I probably purged myself of prejudices that most immigrants never needed to face. Perhaps I felt comfortable merely because everyone's attention was focused on Lionel and Dorothy or Enos and Yvonne, and not on me. Whatever the reason, I enjoyed Jean's friends and looked forward to the weekly parties at Enos's and Yvonne's.

Another reason I looked forward to going out on Friday and Saturday nights was to escape the tension that was building rapidly between Lynn and me. She had developed a willful streak long before I came on the scene—the result, probably, of a broken home and several years on the very edge of poverty—but my appearance certainly didn't help. The Haight-Ashbury drug culture was only thirty miles away in San Francisco and the Free Speech movement was in full flower only minutes farther in Berkeley. When Jean and I got married, despite her dramatic threats of suicide, Lynn settled into a niche of general rebellion. First it was just sullen silence. Then came an assortment of odd friends. (I often overheard her refer to me as "the weirdo that Mom married".) Soon it was late nights out, followed by a new cycle of smoldering resentment when we lectured her about her behavior. Once she went to a Janis Joplin concert at the Fillmore Ballroom in San Francisco and didn't pull in until the next morning. Jean and I became more worried and debated every imaginable strategy of punishment and reward. In my naïveté as a new papa, I brought home a Siamese kitten, which only made me look more "square." Then I tried a German Shepherd puppy named "Brigette" without much success. Lynn progressed to driving our new Plymouth without permission, and Jean and I were getting frantic. I simply didn't know what to do. Looking back, of course, I can see that my mysterious behavior didn't help our relationship, nor did my crew cut and loud Hawaiian shirts. I was in sympathy with the antiwar movement and with her disdain for society's rules and regulations. I worked hard to carry on dinner conversations about art and politics, but to no avail. She seldom spoke at dinner, and I never broached the subject that might have brought us closer together: my dark past. Within two short years she brought home a tall blond young man named David Amherst and announced that he was "Mr. Right." She wanted to get married, and whatever Lynn decided to do, she did. After a nice ceremony in Palo Alto, Lynn moved into a quaint little walk-up apartment in San Francisco. Jean and I could only hope that she had married David for the right reasons, and not just to get out of the house.

Mark, meanwhile, was growing into a quiet, introspective young man who lived in a world of model airplanes, philosophy books, and camping trips. He was three years younger than Lynn and far easier to get along with. Unlike Lynn, Mark had a good relationship with his real father, Harold Bergmann, and kept his last name. In many ways Mark and I were much the same. We were both intensely private people who maintained a wall of mystery around ourselves. Yet we both enjoyed debating about "life" after dinner, and when he wasn't withdrawn or pouting about something, Mark was a wonderful young man. There were many moments when I desperately wished that I could share more of myself with him. When he took up soccer, for example, and became a right-forward on his Cubberly High School team, I longed to tell him that I also had played the same position on my Oberreal team in Schweidnitz. I felt a similar longing when he built a large cage for our German Shepherd puppy out in the garage and painted a sign above it that read: "Stalag 17." What a marvelous opportunity that would have been to tell Mark about prisoner-of-war camps and the years I spent behind the wire. Sadly, I did not say a word and the opportunity to form a bond with my stepson passed unnoticed. Still, we had a warm relationship. I taught him to ski and play tennis, sports in which he excels to this day, and to appreciate the books and viewpoints that influenced me most. Ultimately, what Mark and Lynn gave me was freedom, for Mark's need for privacy and Lynn's rebellious disappearance allowed Jean and me to live our life as we chose. We were able to move where we wanted and embark on whatever adventures presented themselves.

In 1965, however, I was still building shelves for Mark's model planes and a window seat for Lynn's room. One spring day after I had finished constructing a redwood patio and was basking in the sunshine, I turned the page of my newspaper and felt that terrible shock of alarm. I was reading Herb Caen's popular column in the San Francisco *Chronicle,* a daily potpourri of interesting chitchat, when my name jumped out at me. "Georg Gaertner." I thought I was seeing things and read the column slowly.

My eyes followed the length of the column through the hodgepodge of daily gossip in the Bay Area: gallery openings, important people currently in town, and musings about a wife-swapping subculture recently discovered by the *Chronicle*. Then, tucked right in the middle of the column was a trivia entry regarding the existence of a fugitive German prisoner-of-war who escaped from Camp Deming twenty years before—Georg Gaertner. "Wouldn't it be interesting to wonder if Mr. Gaertner, the pride of the Panzers, isn't roaming the streets of San Francisco at this very moment?", Herb Caen speculated. I was stunned! I hadn't seen my real name in print for years and certainly didn't expect to read about myself in the *Chronicle*. And here I was, living less than thirty miles from downtown San Francisco! Mr. Caen then went on for another sentence or two to speculate aloud about Georg's impressions of his fair city: the hilly streets, beautiful parks, the gaudy nightclubs of North Beach, and uniqueness of the city's ethnic communities. I finished reading the column and tried to control my rising panic. Herb's column was read by hundreds of thousands of people, and his interesting tidbits were often the subject of dinner conversations throughout the area. What if everyone began looking for Georg Gaertner? On the other hand, there was no way to link Georg to me. What was I worried about? I just had to stay cautious and keep my nose clean. Still and all, it was a startling intrusion into my new domesticity and a reminder that, trivia or not, I was a federal fugitive. (Ironically, a decade later Herb Caen and I would find ourselves tennis partners in the winning doubles match of the Herb Caen Celebrity Tournament, hosted by my own tennis club.)

Our finances, meanwhile, were taking a sharp downward turn. Business was not going well at the Clark Door Company. The problem was that we were located in the middle of the Peninsula, and the building boom had washed over us to engulf San Jose some fifty miles south. That was just too far for me to go in search of accounts and George Clark, his brother, Alice, and I were struggling to save the jobs of half a dozen expert cabinetmakers and millmen on the payroll. By 1968 we were working hard just to keep the doors open. Luckily I stumbled onto a small enclave of hungry customers in Half Moon Bay, just over the coastal range, which our competitors had somehow overlooked. Jean's job was wearing a bit thin at the same time. As all of us do periodically, she felt that she was overworked and underpaid, and, as the office manager, she had no place to advance to. Fortunately, too, her company selected her to attend a seminar in New York, which perked up her spirits and gave her a renewed sense of accomplishment. For the moment, both her job and mine were limping along, but we could sense a change approaching.

Just when we had adjusted to the temporary tedium of our jobs, we faced a new family problem. Lynn and David broke up, which confirmed our worst fears about her motives in the first place, but we were unprepared for her new direction. First she disappeared into the drug culture of the Haight-Ashbury district. Soon we learned that she had joined a commune in San Francisco, and Jean and I were torn about what to do. If we interfered, Lynn might become even more resentful, and if we didn't, she might cause herself serious harm. Eventually we went to the commune to see for ourselves. The address turned out to be a dark, depressing old house where a dozen pale young kids sat around in moody pursuit of their own "thing." One look at Lynn's thin, pale face and we decided to take her home. I think she had had enough of the hippie life and came home without argument. A few weeks of rest and Jean's good cooking and her color began to return, but not her willingness to live in a structured household. Soon she was off on another generational "bender" that eventually led to a hitchhiking tour through Europe, across Canada and the United States to Big Sur, California.

Our problem with Lynn had little to do with her hippie life-style, but rather her bent toward what seemed to us to be self-destruction. In fact, Jean and I rather enjoyed the youth movement, since it reflected our own attitudes of allowing people to follow their personal life-styles so long as nobody demanded that others do the same. We were attracted to the gentleness of the culture, to its emphasis on peace, love, and racial equality. I found that I liked my longer hair and turtleneck sweaters as Jean did her mini-skirts and twelve-string guitar. It was California in the late 1960s, after all, and Berkeley was less than an hour away. Peace and equality were not generational issues and Jean and I, middle-aged hippies, marched and demonstrated with the best of them. Like any avant-garde movement, we knew we were in the right and were willing to stand behind our beliefs, though why I wasn't concerned about being arrested during a routine demonstration still amazes me. We had paid our dues to society over the years and were only standing up for the principles by which we had always lived. As the hippie movement evolved back into the mainstream so did we, confident that our participation had helped bring about a stronger sense of democracy in America. We also learned that one doesn't have to wear a black turtleneck sweater and a string of wooden beads to live a life of freedom and independence.

BY 1968, CLARK Door Company had finally gone under, and I was fortunate to get a job with a plywood and door outfit in Mountainview. The building boom had definitely bottomed out on the Peninsula, and I knew it was time to move to a new area or consider starting a new career. Jean was also getting restless and was daydreaming about new adventures. Lynn was gone again, and Mark was soon to graduate from Cubberly High School. It seemed like the right time to change. What finally convinced us, I think, was watching Jean's friend Barbara Dolan, a secretary in her office, and her husband, Joe, chuck the hustle and bustle of the Peninsula and open a bar and restaurant in a shopping center in Rio Del Mar. They named it "The Windjammer." Like Jean and I, they were adventurous, though certainly in a bigger league. Both were real risk-takers—high-rolling entrepreneurs who dabbled in such things as million-dollar developments in La Paz, Mexico. They had moved to Rio Del Mar only months before we did, and regardless of our various moves, we remained good friends over the years. One weekend Jean and I drove down the coast past Santa Cruz to Rio Del Mar to give them a helping hand before the opening. I helped Joe hoist an old rowboat over the bar and Jean and Barbara arranged the kitchen supplies. The atmosphere was heavy with salt air and the sounds of sea gulls shrieking overhead made us wonder why we were going back to our routine lives in Palo Alto. I wasn't really surprised several months later when Jean announced that she had found a great house in Rio Del Mar and began a campaign to convince me to move. Frankly, it wasn't difficult. The owner and developer, Dan Succi, was anxious to sell us the home, and the area was an idyllic coastal paradise. We moved into our new place in 1970.

MY JOB IN Mountainview also had finally fallen victim to the construction slump, and I had to find a new job soon. Jean was commuting to her office in Palo Alto every day, a horrible drive through the dangerous curves of old Highway 17. She was approaching her tenth year with Mutual of New York and was talking about retiring. We could live on her salary for awhile, but it was clear that we both were in the market for change. But what could we do in this small, remote coastal village? I drove around the community looking for some evidence of a local industry that might hire me, but saw little to encourage me.

Rio Del Mar was a resort community for the San Francisco peninsula and the wealthy growers who came to escape the heat of the San Joaquin valley. Modern white buildings literally hung on high cliffs above the

Pacific Ocean, and country clubs vied with one another for prestige and affluence. The opening celebrations at exclusive seaside condominiums like "Shore Del Mar" attracted a host of local celebrities. On the fringes of the community were a few motels, their vacancy signs out during the dead winter months, and an old hot dog stand doing a little business with strollers on the beach. Not much in the way of employment for a construction estimator.

I decided that I would fall back on my tennis background and try for a job as a tennis pro at one of the posh country clubs. I literally opened the Yellow Pages and turned to the first entry: Beaver's Swim and Racquet Club. I called and learned that they were indeed in the market for a part-time pro. "But to get the job," they said, "You have to beat our outgoing pro." I hadn't played any serious tennis in years, and I was a bit out of shape. Golf had been our game in Palo Alto. As a matter of fact, I had trouble squeezing into my old white shorts. Still, I had been a tournament-class player a decade before and gave it a try. Mr. and Mrs. Beaver introduced me to Dewey Raburn, Jr., the current pro, whom I had to beat to get the job. He was about my age, in his late 40s, nearing retirement from the telephone company and a fine tennis player. This was going to be a tough match. Guests and players gathered around the court as Dewey and I shook hands and squared off. It turned out to be one of the most grueling matches I remembered playing: two middle-aged veterans (one of whom was decidedly out of shape) who were playing not for money or prestige, but pride. We were more than evenly matched, and each of us had a lifetime of sophisticated moves and tricks to draw upon. He won the first set; then I rallied and won the second. I was approaching the very limits of my endurance. My mind remembered what to do, but my body had forgotten. It was anybody's game as we arrived at the third and final set. Red-faced and panting, I hunched over to begin the last volley. I took a last look at the crowd gathered on the bleachers and to my great delight, I saw Lynn waving her clasped hands over her head for luck. What a surprise! Jean had evidently mentioned that I was playing this match, and Lynn had decided to take a Sunday afternoon drive from San Francisco to cheer me on. After six years of rebellious behavior, this was the most moving symbol of her relationship with me. It was a small gesture, I know, but Lynn's unexpected appearance at my tennis debut dissolved the hostility between us and shored up our relationship for years to come. Her visit was doubly welcome, since I won the final set and the match. I got the job. I was now the tennis pro at Beaver's Swim and Racquet Club, a social position of no small importance in a resort community. Dewey and I, by the way, became fast friends and eventually partners in organizing successful celebrity and international tournaments.

My new job involved providing tennis lessons and lots of socializing. When I wasn't teaching on the courts, I strolled around the lovely terraced grounds and the olympic-sized swimming pool chatting with the guests. It was part of my job and fun besides. It was also relaxing to know that few policemen and FBI agents earned enough money to belong to such an exclusive club and that the chances that any of the guests had ever seen a post office bulletin board were remote. The club did have a problem, however, which was caused by its very exclusiveness. Membership was currently at low ebb, which meant that my teaching schedule was fairly light. That meant that I had lots of spare time. I used that time to develop an interesting project. It began when I discovered that Mr. and Mrs. Beaver had saved every issue of *Tennis* magazine for the last two decades. It occurred to me that these several hundred magazines contained thousands of action-pictures of the top players in the world and that I might be able to isolate some common denominators that could help to make my students better players. I went through every magazine dozens of times checking the body and racquet positions of each photograph to see what they had in common. It took time, but I eventually came up with five composites of the most successful strokes and body positions. I drew slow-motion diagrams of each type of swing, analyzing the shift in position that brought the maximum force and accuracy into play, and wrote an accompanying text for novice and advanced players alike. The final result was an impressive booklet called *Total Tennis* that the club enthusiastically published and distributed widely to other tennis clubs. In retrospect, I must have been feeling supremely confident to have worked so hard to allow my name— and photograph—to reach such wide circulation. It was a risky thing to do. While I was thrilled to know that my tennis insights were useful to many players, I was aghast at my recklessness. I sweated bullets for weeks after the pamphlet appeared all over the Peninsula, wondering who might look at my picture, see a glimmer of recognition, think about it for a few days, and *bingo*! I calmed myself by remembering how much I had changed in twenty-five years. First of all, I was fifty years old, a far cry from the tall, skinny kid who served in Hitler's army. I had sported crew cuts and long hair, gained weight and lost it again, developed wrinkles and a paunch. I was hardly the same man. Moreover, I had recently grown a small Van Dyke beard, a souvenir from a white-water rafting trip down the treacherous Stanislaus River with Jean the summer before. But to put my photograph on the cover of a published pamphlet, beard or not, was dumb.

My FBI files reveal that there had been a substantial dropoff in interest after the capture of my last "comrade," Kurt Westphal, in May of 1964. I had no idea, of course, that I was now the last fugitive German prisoner of war in America, and to tell the truth, I am glad that I didn't know. Whenever I got depressed or frightened by the thought that I had made a slip or was just tired of lying to Jean, I drew strength from the thought that I wasn't alone and that my four other "comrades" were going through the same experiences. I felt they were somehow counting on me. But now I was the last fugitive. More than thirty years had passed since I escaped from Camp Deming, wild-eyed with fear and running across the ghostly white desert toward an approaching freight train. Now here I was: a middle-aged American, married and with a family, and in the early 1970s a tennis pro at one of the most exclusive country clubs in the county. That was the confidence that led me to publish my tennis booklet, photograph and all.

It was true that the FBI had not made much progress since Westphal's capture, but they were far from finished. My wanted poster still hung in every post office and official memos about me moved regularly between Washington and the FBI district office. One encouraging note was beginning to appear in my files: speculation about the possibility that I was dead. Given the fact that two decades had passed since I escaped, the prospect was reasonable. Moreover, if the FBI declared me dead they could close the file. Another case solved. The Albuquerque, New Mexico, office was especially hopeful for such a solution, since it had been made responsible for my case. I was becoming an embarrassment. Several times during the mid-1960s the Albuquerque office petitioned Washington to have me declared dead and removed from their caseload. Finally, they received a brusque memo from J. Edgar Hoover denying their request to sweep the matter under the rug. His only concession was to place my case on an "inactive" status. Consequently, agents continued to routinely check the telephone directories for any spelling of the name "Georg Gaertner" and thoroughly investigated every reported sighting. My wanted posters stayed up. What "inactive status" really meant was that a single verifiable sighting would bring the situation to full alert at any time.

I GOT A real scare in the early spring of 1971. Jean and I had moved again, from Rio Del Mar to a lovely place a dozen miles south at Sand Dollar Beach. Jean had been getting restless and after thinking about it for a couple of weeks, I realized that I was restless as well. Mark was off studying political science at the University of California at Santa Barbara, and Lynn was off to Europe. We only had to worry about the two of us. The move was uneventful, and we continued to commute to work, Jean all the way to Palo Alto every morning and still dreaming of retiring from MONY, and I to the Beavers' Country Club. There was a small community called Aptos between our new home at Sand Dollar and Rio Del Mar, and I developed the habit of stopping at Cabrillo College in Aptos to jog on quiet after-noons. After a few months, I knew many of the joggers and enjoyed meeting old and new friends on the path. One day I was joined by a fellow about my age and we struck up a conversation as we jogged the course across the campus. He was a foreigner; I could tell by his strong accent— probably German or Austrian. He explained that he was in the United States for a month to attend a business conference being held at Cabrillo College and that he was indeed from Germany. I had long ago reached the point where I considered myself totally American and didn't feel the least bit apprehensive about the situation. Still, he kept looking at me, at first out of the corner of his eye, and soon he was really staring. I don't like strangers to take an undue interest in me, and I was beginning to get nervous. "What the hell is on this guy's mind?" I kept wondering to myself. He looked bewildered and seemed to want to talk about something. At the end of the three-mile path we slowed to a walk to catch our breath. He apparently decided to broach whatever subject he had been mulling over. After re-introducing himself and telling me again that he was from Germany, he explained that he had been in the 15th Panzer Division in Africa during the Second World War *(my division!)* and wondered if I might have been there as well. I looked familiar to him and he thought we had met there. I was thunderstruck!! Not in my wildest dreams could I have imagined such a situation! A member of my old Afrika Korps unit?! Here in California?! Thirty years later?! I simply went blank. I should have considered that it was always possible; more than a hundred thousand of us fought under Field Marshal Rommel in North Africa. Thousands more passed through as support troops on temporary assignment. There was always constant movement of men and the appearance of new faces. Doubtless we had crossed paths somewhere, perhaps, in training or enroute

151

through Italy, Yugoslavia, Greece, and Crete; or during any of the battles or lulls of the terrible retreat toward Tunisia. He couldn't quite place me, he said, but he was pretty sure it was in North Africa. "Was I there too?" he asked. It was fortunate that we had just finished running, and I could hide my astonishment by pretending to catch my breath. It was as though my mind had short-circuited. I just couldn't think of the right answer. Finally, I managed to catch my breath long enough to tell him that he must have me mixed up with somebody else. I had never been in North Africa, I told him, and had certainly never been in the German Army! I started to turn away toward my car, and he tried once again, this time taking my arm and saying something in German! I just wanted to get the hell out of there. I pulled loose as politely as I could and strode to my car and sped away. I doubt if my heart stopped racing until I reached my front door in San Dollar half an hour later.

When I finally locked myself in and calmed down, I realized that the danger had passed. He couldn't remember my old name, and I doubt if he heard me say my new name. Even if he did, there was no way to connect "*Kriegsoffizierbewerber* (K.O.B.) Georg Gaertner" of Hitler's Afrika Korps with "Dennis Whiles" of Sand Dollar Beach, California. I also reminded myself that he was only in the United States for the month, and once he left I was perfectly safe. In the meantime, I steered clear of Cabrillo College with a vengeance and even decided to give up jogging for a while on the off chance that I might run into him on some other jogging path. After the panic subsided, I noticed a curious reaction to the whole event: I was almost convinced that he really did have me mixed up with somebody else. A part of me knew that he was talking about me; we were doubtless in the same unit in North Africa. In a way, I was sorry that we couldn't share those experiences once again. They were the best of times and the worst of times—the heroism and defeat that led me to a new life. Above all, it was the high adventure of my young manhood. I would have dearly loved to have discussed those years with a comrade who went through it with me. If that man is today reading these words, I hope he understands why I acted as I did.

At the same time I was annoyed that he would think that I had ever been in the German Army. Thirty years had passed and I was a different person. I had so completely amputated my past that I half-believed he had made a mistake. I was almost insulted that he would think that I—a devoted American—would have served in the *Wehrmacht*. I didn't even understand the German words he was speaking! As curious as it may be, I was literally a different person. Still, it was a terrific shock to bump into an Afrika Korps veteran who remembered me from the old days even if there was no immediate danger. I only wished that I could have told Jean why I was so shaken and introspective when she came home from work.

WORK, IN FACT, was becoming a problem for both of us. Jean wanted to retire "at the first opportunity," which meant when I found a job that would support us. Until then, she grudgingly agreed to carry us a little longer. It was time for me to decide. We both enjoyed the social prestige of my job as the tennis pro at Beaver's and unashamedly gloried in the local limelight. I also relished the opportunity to publish my pamphlet on *Total Tennis*. On the other hand, community status didn't pay the bills. I was certainly never going to become a millionaire this way. Jean and I began discussing the possibilities of quitting our jobs and going into something local and lucrative.

We found what we were looking for at the exclusive Aptos Country Club. It was the "in" place for wealthy golfers as Sugar Bowl was for skiers. The club catered to people who shunned the opulent golf courses on the Monterey Peninsula in favor of a smaller club with a personal touch. Most returned year after year. What Aptos did not have, however, was a tennis club. Tennis was becoming more popular by the day. Given this growing popularity but few available public courts, Jean and I felt that it would be a perfect place to start a racquet club. They had five hundred acres of dormant real estate where we visualized a pro shop, restaurant, and rows of tennis courts. The potential was clearly there, and with my tennis skills and Jean's business ability, we couldn't lose. What we needed, however, was the enthusiastic support of the Aptos Country Club and, from whatever source, some investment capital.

Aptos, it turned out, was delighted with our proposal. They knew we would bring in business. Aside from the courts at Cabrillo College and the few public courts downtown, our new tennis club would be the only place in town. Aptos would gain new members, not to mention the profits from a pro shop, the restaurant and bar. They could sell lots to wealthy home builders. Moreover, if we could encourage tennis organizations to hold their matches and tournaments at Aptos, the reputation of the club would benefit. The other reason they were so cooperative was that the manager of Aptos, Boyd Lang turned out to be a friend of mine! Boyd had once developed a huge housing project near Novato, in Marin County, and had been my account when I worked for Herb. "Great idea," he said. "It's fine with us; see if you can find some investment money." The money came from a new acquaintance, Walter Field, a wealthy young man whose main interests were tennis and banking. It didn't take me long to show him how the two passions could be combined. Before long Jean and I were in business. I gave notice at Beaver's, and Jean gratefully retired from MONY.

WE OPENED A small shop at the entrance to the lodge, which Jean named the "Tennis Scene." We hurriedly stocked it with tennis fashions, imported Austrian sweaters, courtesy of Bill and Fred Klein, and a few rackets and warm-up suits. I tried to introduce my aluminum "Dennis Racquet" through my shop as well, but it still didn't take off. Our little tennis world quickly became a beehive of activity. Dewey Raburn came by and joined, as did Lowell and Yvonne Welch and many of our other friends. Soon we were offering a variety of instruction packages and even sponsored sports fashion shows. By the end of our first year, I was teaching classes totaling hundreds of people, mainly youngsters, and during the off-season winter months, I taught many of the same kids ski courses organized on the sand dunes of the local beaches. When Mark had college vacations, he came to work as my assistant instructor in both sports. Things were going so well that I had to worry about pacifying the large golfing population of the club, which felt it was being eclipsed by our intrusion. Jean and I tried to mend fences at every opportunity, participating in their golfing tournaments and fashion shows.

Jean and I reveled in the social life of the community. We entertained regularly and were invited to every party, sports tournament, and condominium opening. New friendships abounded. Ed and Marge Fawcett, for example. Ed was a retired Volvo dealer and an accomplished oil painter, later to become my art teacher. Marge was an outgoing bubbly blonde who enthusiastically helped Jean with fashion shows. They had a beautiful winter condominium in Hawaii, at Lahaina on the island of Maui, and after several joint trips there with them, eventually convinced us to move to Hawaii permanently.

We also developed a close friendship with Lee Hill, a tennis player and real estate developer in Rio Del Mar and Pebble Beach. Lee invited us regularly to play at the elegant Pebble Beach Country Club, where we could mingle with the celebrities who retreated there to escape the pressures of public life: people like Clint Eastwood, Merv Griffin, Gene Hackman, and Efram Zimbalist, Jr. Another important friend was Peter Herb, the executive director of the Northern California Tennis Association. Peter later appointed me the director of the Junior Davis Cup team of Santa Cruz County and sanctioned the Junior and Pro Tournaments that were held at my tennis club. I had arrived. I even basked in the appearance of front-page spreads in the local Watsonville newspapers, *The Pajaronian* and the *Sun Press,* which lauded us as "The Pace-Setters of the Year." Georg Gaertner was a million miles away.

It was in this rarefied atmosphere that I crossed paths with Joe Chinchiolo, the cherry wholesaler from Stockton, for whom I had worked nearly twenty-five years before, loading cherries into boxcars for shipment to New York. He recognized me immediately as "Peter Peterson," the Norwegian immigrant lumberjack, and, of course, I recognized him. I lived in terror for weeks, waiting for the moment when the FBI would walk into my tennis shop as they did with poor Reinhold Pabel in his Chicago bookstore back in 1953 and arrest me in front of my friends. It took a month or more before I felt safe enough to look up at each new customer without fearing that he would hold out a badge and quietly suggest that we walk to a waiting car. Luckily, nothing happened and after a month or so, I put the whole matter out of my mind. It was time to get back to the high life.

The owners of the Aptos Country Club (reportedly the Teamsters Union) were genuinely impressed with the success of our tennis activity. Boyd Lang had since moved on and was replaced by a new management team. To my initial joy, they decided that we were doing well enough to make a separate tennis center. Our new name was the Aptos Seascape Racquet Club, and the management embarked on an impressive project designed to attract national championship tournaments and wealthy resort homeowners. Aptos was run by people who went first class! The new facilities included six regular tennis courts; a flood-lit sunken championship arena with bleacher seating for 1,100 people; a 75-foot junior AAU-size swimming pool; a bar and restaurant for private members; locker rooms with whirlpool baths and sauna; and an entire building devoted to the pro shops of the new tennis director: Dennis Whiles! Huge bulldozers were brought in and the groundbreaking ceremony took place at the beginning of the summer, 1971. What a festival. Tennis celebrities and socialites came from miles around to enjoy the special exhibition matches by such luminaries as Barry MacKay, former leading ranked U.S. tennis pro; Gil Rodriquez, former NCAA tennis champion and the pro at Hawaii Kai Racquet Club; my pal Dewey Raburn, director of the Northern California Tennis Association; and yours truly. A bunch of area sports reporters were also there, but I wasn't concerned. It was hardly smart behavior for a man who was sought by the FBI but I was just having too much fun to care about it.

In September, Peter Herb arranged for our first sanctioned tournament. This was an important milestone at Seascape because a tournament authorized by the U.S. Lawn Tennis Association made the scores official and players eligible to compete toward state and national championships. The Aptos Corporation put up an awesome $30,000 in prize money, and we hosted the First Annual Seascape Senior Doubles Gold Championship. We were on our way. No sooner was that tournament over than Dewey, Peter Herb, and I organized the Santa Cruz Junior Davis Cup Championships. More celebrities, entertainment, and sports reporters. The next tournament materialized from an unexpected direction and turned out to be humorously ironic. It also created an incident that started the deterioration of my relationship with the Aptos management.

One day I was approached by a well-dressed older man with a gorgeous starlet on his arm. He introduced himself as Al Haber from Santa Cruz, and the doll as the future Mrs. Haber. "What I want to talk to you about is you and I putting on a Celebrity Tournament at Seascape, with the proceeds going to charity. You do the organizing," he said, and with a broad wink to the actress on his arm, added, "and I'll furnish the celebrities." Talk about luck!! Here was a guy who wanted to help underwrite a major tournament at my club and with me as the organizer. It was almost *my* tournament!! Jean was apprehensive about the responsibility of such a huge project, but the challenge was too seductive. Al Haber and I talked it over and shook hands. We set the dates for May 5–7, 1972.

First, we set up a committee to select a celebrity to bear the name of the tournament. It had to be a Californian, of course, and someone known to play an excellent game of tennis. The committee selected Herb Caen, of the San Francisco *Chronicle,* highly respected and a well-known tennis enthusiast. How ironic. Almost ten years before, he wrote about Georg Gaertner walking the streets of San Francisco; now he would actually meet him. The charity we chose was the Dominican Hospital in Santa Cruz, and, of course, they were delighted. We unleashed a publicity blitz that brought in droves of local celebrities: TV personalities and newspapers columnists, and even football stars, from as far as San Francisco. We enlisted the help of a number of former Davis Cup players, and the general public enthusiastically paid $5 per person to watch them play in exhibition matches. Even though I was the resident pro, I saw no reason not to enter the tournament with a celebrity partner. That decision, while certainly legal, led to a problem. Herb Caen and I won. The management was furious. All that publicity and expense wasted, they contended, because the tournament looked rigged. Nobody else seemed the least bit concerned. There was no prize money, after all, and all the profits went to the hospital. Nonetheless the management seemed soured by the event, and we began to avoid each other.

THE APTOS MANAGEMENT was not the only source of anger in my life. Jean was getting angry too. While I was out on the courts, poor Jean was stuck running the pro shop and worrying about things like inventories and sales tax. She was supporting me, as always, and getting damned irritated about it. We had also been working side-by-side every day for more than a year, and the strain was beginning to show.

I didn't know it at the time, but she was also growing suspicious about my past. A lot of things didn't jibe, and they were beginning to add up. It began with my slip-up at the wedding about not having been married before as I had originally told her. Then, a physical examination through her MONY insurance revealed that I had once had serious cases of both diptheria and pneumonia, neither of which I had ever told her about. The medical report also discussed the remnants of a nasty break on my shin, which I had also neglected to mention. I just didn't seem to have a past, and it was getting to her. I knew it, but what could I do? I knew our relationship was drifting toward trouble but didn't want to open the gates to a full-blown crisis. Instead, I made believe that the growing tension was simply due to our overwork. If there really was a problem, I figured it was only temporary.

Meanwhile, life went on, a whirlwind of teaching tennis, organizing tournaments, and playing exhibition matches to promote Aptos Seascape. One match turned out to be unique: it was the only time I intentionally lost. My friend Walter Field, the banker, invited me to be his doubles partner at his annual alumni tournament at Stanford. Walter took Stanford University as seriously as he took tennis and banking, so I was honored to have been asked. We played well together and made it to the finals. Walter was overjoyed. He was a tough competitor and loved to win. He was even happier to be winning at his alumni reunion. We had about an hour's break before the final match, which we stood an excellent chance of winning. While waiting, I decided to stroll around the hallowed halls of Stanford and eventually found myself standing in front of the large brass plaque on which the names of each year's alumni winners were engraved. I visualized the next entry: "1972—Walter Field and Dennis Whiles." Suddenly I felt so guilty. I was struck by the permanence of what was about to happen. Walter and I were about to win the alumni doubles championship and our names would be forever linked on this imposing plaque. It would have been sacred to Walter. The prospect of tarnishing his moment made me squirm. What if I was caught some day? I might become an embarrassment to Walter. My arrest would certainly shock my friends and tennis colleagues—not to mention my wife—but I always felt that once they knew the circumstances they would get over it. I think that Walter would also understand, but it would have blemished his winning moment at Stanford.

As I walked back to begin the finals, I started to feel sick. It was psychological, of course. I didn't want to win. I know that I talked myself into it, but I really thought I was ill. I could hardly lift my racket to serve. We lost, although we both knew that our opponents were not as good as we. Walter was bitterly disappointed, but forgave me. I hope he'll still be as understanding after reading these words. Incidently, while I was congratulating our opponents directly after the match a photographer from *Sports Illustrated* appeared. He wanted a few pictures of the tournament winners for the next issue. "This will be seen from coast to coast," he assured us, and politely asked if Walter and I might step aside for a moment while he took the picture. Just hearing the words "will be seen from coast to coast" was enough for me. I graciously moved away and silently thanked heaven that I had lost the tournament.

In September 1972, we hit the big time. After lengthy negotiations with the Northern California Tennis Association and the national U.S. Lawn Tennis Association, Seascape was allowed to host its first international tournament: the Grand Prix. This was serious stuff. Players from all over the world competed for the tournament championship, including several from behind the Iron Curtain. Among the most impressive entries was a rising young Swedish star named Bjorn Borg (who did not win the top money), Jan Kodes from Czechoslovakia, and such well-known American players as Dennis Ralston and Bob Lutz. It was the professional gathering of the season in northern California. My role this time was as the official referee. Everything went great until I was called in to settle a court dispute and all eyes were suddenly on me. During one of the matches another player from Czechoslovakia became outraged at the umpire's call. He threw his racket on the ground and called the umpire (who happened to be black), "You black son of a bitch!" Suddenly the whole tournament froze. Tennis is an aristocratic sport where etiquette and gallantry are as important as skill. Winners and losers shake hands over the net at the end. Throwing one's racquet and insulting the umpire during a match—especially a sanctioned international tournament—is a gross violation of accepted behavior. The more so when the insult is a racial slur. The official was understandably outraged and demanded that the player be thrown out of the match. The Czech claimed that he didn't speak any English and that the words he shouted didn't mean anything to him. The umpire refused to budge on the call. Both turned to me as the official referee and suddenly sports reporters, club officials, and the packed bleachers all focused on my decision. This was my nightmare. Several thousand people were breathlessly awaiting a decision that was bound to outrage one side or the other. I could imagine the sports headlines: "International incident occurred today at Aptos Seascape between a black American umpire and a Czech champion: the official ruling was made by Referee Dennis Whiles, a fugitive German prisoner of war!" After consulting with both the Czech and the umpire, I ruled that the umpire's original decision was correct but that the Czech's insult did not warrant dismissal from the tournament. I thought it was the best decision under the circumstances. While my ruling was later supported by the national office, I waited in anguish for our photos to appear in the papers. A few papers carried the story, but gratefully there were no further ramifications.

Despite all the tournaments and publicity for Aptos Seascape, my relations with the club management were deteriorating fast. I believed that one of the management team saw my efforts to bring in major tournaments as high-handed, and that he was still annoyed by my having won the finals match of the Herb Caen Celebrity Tournament. But I suspect that the real problem was that business had fallen off and fewer homeowners were buying lots at Aptos. Perhaps the tennis club was getting too popular and those in authority were under pressure from the club's powerful golf lobby.

159

Whatever the reason, I felt that I was in a narrowing chute. There were already rumors that they were on the lookout for a younger (and more subservient) tennis director. In mid-1973 it was announced, imperiously it seemed to me, that they had hired a traveling pro, a young Davis Cup player by the name of Eric Van Dillon. I felt sure that I was in for a squeeze play. Not that it was unusual for a prestigious country club to have a traveling tennis or golf pro in addition to its resident pro; in fact, it was a good idea. A traveling pro, especially one with Van Dillon's solid qualifications and public appeal, could only enhance the reputation of his home club as he participated in tournaments around the country. What bothered me was that it was done without my knowledge. Such a breach of sports etiquette confirmed my fear that my days at Aptos were numbered.

Consequently, I was grateful when I was unexpectedly invited to participate in a major tennis match, the Alamo Pro-Am Fireman's Fund Tournament, at the Alamo Country Club at Walnut Creek. It was impressive to be invited to play at such a prestigious match under any circumstances, but because of my relationship with club management, it was vital that I demonstrate my ability and take every opportunity to enhance my reputation. The Alamo Pro-Am Tournament turned out even better than I had hoped. I was playing in the company of the best professional players in California and was assured of several invitations to still more tournaments in the future. At Alamo I also got a chance to play with Robert Stack. When Jean and I had lunch with him, his wife, Rosemarie, and Mrs. Edgar Bergen afterward, I reminded him that I had once cooked his hamburgers, twenty-five years before, at the ski lodge at Sugar Bowl. To my astonishment he remembered me and Tim, the bartender.

One invitation that followed was to the impressive James MacArthur Celebrity Tournament in Hawaii the following summer, 1974, where I was to be, ahem, the tournament tennis coordinator. Jean and I left on our annual vacation in January that year to beautiful Hawaii, buoyed up with optimism. Surely, the management of Aptos couldn't justify replacing me now. After several wonderfully relaxing weeks in Hawaii, we returned to the tension of Aptos Seascape. I was reasonably sure that the management was pacified by my recent tennis successes. I looked forward to a pleasant and challenging new year.

The first important sports event upon our return was the annual Aptos Country Club Awards Ceremony. It was a fun weekend that culminated in the presentation of the awards. At the end of the awards ceremony, one of the managers rose to make a special announcement: Aptos Seascape was pleased to announce the name of its new resident tennis pro: Henry Kamakana, the number one ranked player in northern California! There was a smattering of applause across the packed bleachers. Jean and I were stunned! I had just been fired! As the crowds realized what had happened, a number of people looked toward me with perplexed expressions on their faces: why I hadn't mentioned my departure before? Jean and I were still in shock and could only shrug back in bewilderment. An angry exchange with my boss afterward proved fruitless. Kamakana was the new tennis pro and I was out. No reason; no explanation. We went home in smoldering fury to consider our future. Clearly, there was no way to remain at Aptos. My pride would never allow me to plead, and management wouldn't have me anyway. The only consolation was that most of my friends would quit in a huff and I hoped that the club would feel the loss of business. I also took some comfort in the fact that I was being replaced by one of the best. Henry Kamakana was a top-flight player from Hawaii, whose father, incidentally, was a highly respected teaching pro at the Mauna Kea Resort until well into his seventies. If I had to be replaced, I figured that they had to go to the top of the ranks to do it.

ONCE THE SHOCK and embarrassment had passed, we had to do some serious planning. It was clear that it was time to move to a new area. Neither of us felt comfortable there any longer. And where would we get new jobs? We liked our tennis lifestyle and had proved that we were good at it. We had created a tennis club from scratch. We had maintained a successful pro shop, organized major tournaments, provided lessons, and orchestrated well-attended sports events and fashion shows. We brought in a lot of business. Now that we had the experience, Jean and I decided we could do the same thing somewhere else. Moreover, since we could avoid many of our earlier mistakes, we could do it better.

Money wouldn't be an immediate problem. We would make a substantial profit on our beautiful house in Sand Dollar Beach, since the property values in the area were skyrocketing. The kids were long gone, so we were entirely mobile. Mark had graduated from Santa Barbara and was learning the hotel business (he was the front desk manager at a Holiday Inn). Lynn had drifted to Boulder, Colorado, after several years of self-searching at Big Sur, and was happy with her new husband, Bob Bauer. There didn't seem to be anything holding us back. The big question was: where would we go?

Jean spread the maps on the kitchen table and we began the exciting process of selecting our new home. Our goal was a wealthy resort community where tennis was popular and courts were scarce. We settled on the nearby town of Salinas, some fifty miles south of us, not far from Monterey. After discussing all the pros and cons, we agreed: Salinas it is! A new adventure! Rubbing our hands in excitement we embarked on the familiar routine. We put the house on the market and sold it quickly for even more than we hoped. Now we had investment capital of our own. We put our belongings in storage until we found a new house and jobs in Salinas. Now came the hard part: we had to say good-bye again. Our friends at Aptos Seascape threw a lovely farewell party for us, and several hundred members turned out to wish us well in our new venture. We made plans to see many of them again on our new courts in Salinas.

As we drove south from Aptos on the coastal highway toward Salinas, Jean and I chatted aimlessly about what our new house might be like, and our future neighbors and friends. We talked about old friends and the conversation drifted to our recent vacation in Hawaii. What a tropical paradise! We would be there again for the James MacArthur Celebrity Tournament in the summer, and we were already looking forward to it. But that was almost five months away, we groaned. Wouldn't it be terrific if we could go sooner? Think of all the fun we could have until the tournament. The restaurants and the breathtaking scenery and the tennis opportunities and the intriguing ethnic cultures and the. . . Suddenly we looked at each other. Why were we going to Salinas? We really wanted to go to Hawaii! We pulled over by the side of the highway and hesitatingly considered the prospect. We had no commitments in Salinas; our hosue was sold and we had enough money to live on for a while without working; the kids were busy with their own lives; and we really loved Hawaii. Should we do it? A long pause. We both broke into smiles and that said it all. We turned the car around and drove up to San Francisco. Several days later we left for Honolulu, and we remained in Hawaii for ten years. What began that day in the spring of 1974 as an exciting adventure, eventually took us to the collapse of our marriage, the brink of divorce, and, ultimately, to the writing of this book.

SEVEN

H AWAII IS JUST like the travel brochures describe it, only better. No folder can describe the welcome feeling of coming upon a string of islands rising out of the Pacific Ocean more than 2,500 miles from the West Coast. After long hours of staring at the flat, blue ocean below, they suddenly appear out of nowhere. The distant spots become eight distinct mountainous islands: large, green, and lush. The capital, Honolulu, is located on Oahu, one of the smaller islands near the upper end of the chain. From Oahu it is 55 miles to the next link in the chain, Molokai; 84 miles to Maui; and 169 miles to the "Big Island," Hawaii. Scattered among them are the smaller islands: Lanai ("The Pineapple Isle"), Kauai ("The Garden Isle"), and the rocky crag at the northwestern tip of the chain, justly named Niihau, "The Forbidden Isle." Together they make up a tropical paradise as startling and beautiful as it must have first appeared to the great explorer of the Pacific, Captain James Cook, who discovered them in 1778 and named them the Sandwich Islands. The discovery of the native kingdom attracted an army of intrepid missionaries, sailors, and immigrants, many of whom paid a high price for life in paradise. Captain Cook was killed by the Hawaiian natives the year after his arrival. At the time when Napoleon was emperor of Europe, Hawaii was ruled by the powerful King Kamehameha I, who united the islands; when America was on the verge of the automobile age, Queen Lydia Liliuokalani lived in a grass hut. Hawaii became of strategic importance in the 1890s and was annexed by the United States in 1898. Basking

163

in sunshine almost year-round, the Hawaiian islands contain breathtaking mountain roads and tropical rain forests, beaches with unending assortments of beautiful bodies, and high cliffs where one can watch humpback whales frolicking a short distance out to sea. A paradise. People in Ames, Iowa, wait their whole lives to come to Hawaii for a two-week vacation, and TV contestants hold their breaths in the hope that the toothy M.C. will announce that they have won THE TRIP!! Hawaii is everyone's dream vacation, and Jean and I were going to go there.

We arrived with plenty of money and no particular schedule. My only obligation was the James MacArthur Celebrity Tournament during the summer. We began like any tourists, starting with Honolulu, Pearl Harbor, Diamond Head, and Waikiki Beach. From there we went to the island of Kauai and roamed the Waimea Canyon and tried to count the reported forty shades of green that grow on the slopes of the Waialeale Mountains. We traveled to Maui and strolled the streets of Lahaina Town for a look at what whaling life in the 1800s was like. We gawked at the posh resorts at Kaanapali and Kapalua, drove along the spectacular coast roads and past the sugar cane plantations, and trekked up a 10,000 foot dormant volcano. Next came the big island of Hawaii where we marveled at the black sand beaches and the snowcapped mountains, the fields of orchids and anthuriums, and the original culture of Polynesia. It was all so beautiful I could scarcely believe we were going to actually live here. By the beginning of summer we figured that it was time to settle down; we chose a new development at Makaha, about thirty miles north of Honolulu on the remote side of the island of Oahu. It was a native Hawaiian community, and we were among the few Caucasians living there. We bought a lovely twelfth-floor condominium on the edge of one of the world's greatest beaches at Turtle Bay.

I often sat on the balcony and stared out at the fabulous sunsets beyond Makaha's Lahi Lahi Point and considered the events that had brought me here. Had I really spent my childhood in that remote Silesian town? Was I related to the soldier in the Afrika Korps, hungry and exhausted after months of battle, who sometimes passed through my dreams? It was even becoming hard to recall that I once labored in the migrant worker camps of the San Joaquin Valley. Where might I be today, I wondered, if things had been different? One thing was certain: if I hadn't escaped from that prisoner-of-war compound at Deming, New Mexico, I would be living under the Russians. My old town of Schweidnitz was now part of northern

Poland. Poland! Of all the places in the world where I could imagine spending my life, communist Poland was definitely the least attractive. I thought sadly about my parents and my older brother and sister, Paul and Lotte. Their lives had been filled with war and deprivation. They had lived under the Kaiser, the Nazis, and finally the Soviets. They represented an entire tragic generation of modern Europe whose world had been shattered by World War I, crippled by the catastrophic inflation of the 1920s, followed by the Great Depression, Hitler, and World War II. Even after the war Europe offered little promise of security as the survivors faced new tribulations of devastation and foreign occupation. My family was representative of millions of Europeans whose lives were scarred by war, upheaval, and fear. Yet, they had saved me—cast me to safety. They had prepared me for survival, very much like the opening scene of the Superman story when the parents put their infant into a rocket as their planet erupts around them. They encouraged the very skills that I needed to start life anew. My father even paid to have me take some driving lessons, although at the time I was mystified because we didn't own a car. They were pleased that I decided to study English. It was as though my family had spared me the fate of their generation. I always felt that they would have been proud of my successful survival in America and that they would have understood my need to cut all emotional ties the day I decided to escape from Camp Deming. I knew that they wouldn't have wanted me to risk my safety in America by tracking their whereabouts after the war. Perhaps their mail was being watched and a letter from me might have led to my arrest. I cannot help but think that they would have been disappointed at such carelessness. They had thrown me to safety, and I would have compromised everything over an unnecessary postcard. Who knows what would have happened to me if I had stayed in the POW camp and allowed myself to be repatriated to Schweidnitz. One thing was sure: I wouldn't be sitting out here on the balcony of my high-rise condominium watching the last rays of a magnificent sunset in Hawaii.

JEAN AND I had no trouble adjusting to our new lives in Hawaii. Although we didn't need the money yet, Jean decided to look for some work. She had no difficulty landing an interesting job in the Hawaiian Department of Social Services. This time, instead of caring for the migrant workers of California, she was responsible for providing social services to the shrinking population of native Hawaiians, most of whom lived in our community

165

of Makaha and in Nanakuli. Working among the locals she developed a special relationship with Hawaii that tourists never experience. I, on the other hand, was not ready for a 9-to-5 job, and since we had the money, I decided to pursue tennis and painting instead. I developed a daily routine of playing tennis with local champions like old Mr. Tamura, known as "Mr. Tennis" of nearby Waianae, his son Cliff, and Vernon Daily, a former U.S. Army tennis champion, and one of the first pros at Honolulu's famous Royal Hawaiian Hotel. Then came a swim at Makaha Beach; and finally, I spent the late afternoon learning to paint in oils, aided by lessons from my friend Ed Fawcett who had since opened an art gallery on Front Street in Lahaina on Maui. I sat out on the balcony (called a *lanai* in the islands) sketching and enjoying the sunsets. Weekends Jean and I spent together: driving through the tropical rain forests or eating *poi* at a native *luau*. We quickly grew to love the Hawaiians and their relaxed life style. I felt especially comfortable since everyone had an accent and most didn't care for the *federales* any more than I did.

Before I knew it, the James MacArthur Celebrity Tournament had arrived. As the costar of TV's popular show "Hawaii Five-O" and a fine tennis player in his own right, "Danno's" name added luster to those of dozens of other major celebrities who graciously lent their time and enthusiasm for charity: MacDonald Carey, Claudine Longet, Mike Conners, Paul Lukas, and many more. Lloyd Bridges and I played as doubles partners. Ten years later I bumped into him at the Aspen Pro-Am Tournament and we reminisced about our match in Hawaii. What fun to have someone like Lloyd Bridges recognize you among hundreds of star-struck ticket-holders and reach out for a handshake.

BY THE SPRING of 1975 our nest egg was nearing bottom and I felt it was time to consider a job. There were few opportunities as a tennis pro for one of the major hotels or racquet clubs, so I found myself leaning toward my old work in the construction trade. There wasn't much glamor, but it paid more than tennis lessons and occasional tournament prizes. I was also getting leery of my high profile; I was taking too many chances. It was time to find a new challenge and a well-paying job. There was another reason that we needed money: the kids had each decided to join us in Hawaii. Mark was attracted by our description of life in Hawaii and felt that the opportunities in the hotel business were better than on the Mainland. We were delighted to see him. He went to work at the exclusive Japanese-owned Makaha Inn as a "Bell Activities Person" (called a bellboy in the old days) and within a year and a half was promoted to assistant manager—an impressive position in a resort state that lives on tourism and pride of service. Then Lynn and her husband, Bob, and their infant son, Michael—our wonderful new grandchild!—arrived from Boulder. We spent our remaining savings on a condominium for them at nearby Aiea and gloried in having our little brood around us once again. If we were hoping for permanence we were wrong. Two years later Lynn and Bob split up, and she took young Michael back to Colorado. She eventually married Steve Grosz whom I am pleased to report has turned out to be the goal she spent so many years pursuing. They have a solid and loving relationship and still live harmoniously in Colorado. Mark remained in Hawaii for a couple of more years before the lure of business advancement drew him to Colorado as well. When they both appeared in Hawaii in 1975, however, it was clear that I needed to find a good-paying job.

One day I noticed from the balcony that there was some construction starting right below us. I wandered down to take a look and found that some Chinese developers were going to build six hundred living units for a new subdivision called Holiday Plantation. Since many in the community, mostly native Hawaiians, were unemployed, I figured that my experience as a millman-estimator might get me in. I walked into the construction office and asked for an application. To my surprise the project manager's name was familiar. He was Bob Brubeck, brother of the famous jazz musician Dave Brubeck whom I knew of when he played at the Black-hawk Club in San Francisco. We reminisced about the old days over a cup of coffee and after listening to my work history with Herb, the Clark Door Company, and the rest, he waved aside any need for a formal application and made me the project's small tool purchaser. I was very pleased; first, because I was able to avoid the dreaded application form, and second, it was a position of some importance considering the hundreds of carpenters and construction workers who were employed on the development. They all required a wide array of tools, and it was my responsibility to anticipate their needs and buy the tools at the best price. Everything had to be stored, maintained, and accounted for. It was a challenging job, all right, but the paperwork was killing. Besides, once the tools were bought, and I set up a system to identify them and keep pilferage under control, my task was basically over. I convinced Bob to assign me to other tasks. Over the next months I held a variety of positions, eventually rising to safety inspector, a dangerous job considering the high winds, volcanic rock, and pace of construction. In fact, to counteract a rash of unusual accidents, we arranged a ceremony so the gods could bless the construction site! When the Holiday Plantation development was finished, I had the business contacts to look for another project.

My next job was bigger, as I had hoped, but also scarier. I hired on with a Milwaukee-based construction firm called Towne Realty Company, which had a government contract to build two thousand living units at the Navy base at Puuloa. My responsibilities were extremely demanding, and I found out that my predecessor had quit in despair. I had to supply the exact amount of lumber and material for each unit, a mind-boggling task that involved the calculation of thousands of board-feet cut to the last inch. If the carpenters were short one board-foot of lumber they couldn't finish the house on schedule; two or three feet of lumber beyond their needs meant a reprimand from the project supervisor about wastefulness and tight budgets. I practically lived in a huge trailer parked on the construction site, surrounded by blueprints, adding machines, slide rule, and material supply books. Part of my success at the job was due to a young boom operator named Rudy who often alerted me to unseen problems, double-checked my calculations, and sometimes moved lumber around if I came up short at one unit or delivered too much to another. Interestingly, Rudy was a German immigrant who had studied some engineering at school and who attacked mathematics problems with a doggedness for which the Germans are famous. He was anxious to make a go of it in America, and we often found time for small talk. I never revealed my story to him, of course, and listened in silence when he told me about the devastation of the postwar years. He had no intention of giving up and returning to the limited opportunities in Germany—and neither did I. Although Rudy never knew how much we had in common, we made a good team and stayed together on the next several jobs. Our favorite expression during that time—we said it laughingly—was "Let's *blitz* them with materials."

The frightening part of the job was that we were working on a contract for the government. The construction site was on the outskirts of the naval base and was hopping with sentries; there were plenty of checkpoints, chain-link fences, and identification cards. It was nerve-racking from morning to night and probably accounted for the substantial amounts of time I spent locked in the trailer with my calculations. No sooner did we finish the units at Puuloa than Towne Realty announced a new contract. We were all moved to the Army post at Schofield Barracks in the middle of Oahu to build twenty-five-hundred living units, and the terror began again. More military police, ID cards, and chain-link fence. Since we were working outside the perimeter of the main post I didn't worry about a direct confrontation, though the possibility of a serious run-in was ever-present. I just prayed that my luck would hold out.

Things were not going well at home. Lynn had separated from Bob and left with Michael for Colorado. We had no sooner adjusted to being grandparents when the chance to practice that evaporated. Doug was making plans to leave Hawaii as well, though it was with confidence and enthusiasm in the future. Jean was totally immersed in the problems of the native Hawaiians and Samoans and had little time to listen to my problems. On the few occasions when I tried to explain my fears of working around the military bases she would shake her head in bewilderment. In retrospect I can't blame her: what normal adult was frightened of harmless sentries and chain-link fence? Why didn't I tell her the truth now? We'd been married almost fifteen years and we knew each other as well as we were probably going to. I could no longer believe that she would leave me because of it, although to tell the truth our relationship was strained enough so that I doubt if I would have been distraught if she had. Then why couldn't I sit her down on a quiet Sunday afternoon and unravel the story of my past? I think it was now an issue of embarrassment. I didn't want to look foolish or criminal. I had worked too hard to create a heroic image to see it shattered. No, I decided, I would tough it out, sentries and all.

I had boxed myself in and couldn't seem to find a way out. My anxiety continued to increase at work as the jobs brought me into closer contact with the military. We did a job, for example, near Kole Kole Pass, where the Japanese planes crossed over Oahu when they attacked Pearl Harbor on December 7, 1941. Marine guards were stationed at Kole Kole Pass, and I was checked daily as I went to and from the construction site. The guards were seldom the same and each insisted on a thorough examination of my company ID. On more than one occasion my anxiety erupted as anger at being checked again, and I often took the long way around to avoid trouble. Jean, naturally, couldn't understand why I was being so sensitive about a few questions. (Ah, to be an American and not to be frightened of the authorities!) It was not only the military who concerned me. As our company took on larger and larger contracts, we often hired laborers who were ex-cons or who had police problems of their own. That meant that we were sometimes visited by parole officers and detectives who wanted to talk to one of our workers. I was becoming a nervous wreck and going home to Jean didn't help.

I thought that changing jobs might do the trick. By now I had a good reputation in the construction industry, and when we finished the project at Kole Kole Pass, I decided to look for another job. Jean was perturbed that I would leave such a good job with Towne Realty but shrugged it off and went back to her clients. I applied for work at Morrison-Knudsen, one of the ten largest construction companies in the U.S. They were embarking on an ambitious project to build some three thousand military homes in a vast shallow volcanic crater, and I was made responsible for all the lumber required. This was a monster project and one that again brought me uncomfortably close to the military. It was much the same story: long weeks burrowed in the trailer office furiously calculating from my native metric system to feet and yards, and trying to look casual when passing through the guard posts or when I suddenly ran into a parole officer looking for one of my crew. On one occasion I ran afoul of the Marine commandant. It began as a minor disagreement and escalated out of control. He felt that I was challenging his authority on the construction site. I know that I was simply tired and overworked. Whatever the reason, I went home and told Jean the story. I asked for her help. Now here was something she could get her teeth into. Outraged at the way the "damn military" had treated her husband, she called the commandant and read him the riot act. California girls are like that. While I felt like a high school kid whose mother calls the principal on his behalf, I basked in safety at hearing her shout into the telephone about what steps she intended to take if he ever interfered with her husband's work again. By the time Jean slammed down the phone on a Marine colonel who probably wished he was back fighting the Vietcong, I was surer than ever that I just couldn't tell her the truth about my past. I needed her strength and support, her innocent outrage on my behalf, and her love. The fact that the commandant gave me a wide berth from then on only convinced me that I couldn't do anything to break her faith in me. The construction project eventually ended on schedule, and we all waited for the final report from company headquarters in Boise, Idaho. It was our "report card," so to speak, which evaluated our performance and adherence to our budgets. A bad report would seriously damage our reputations in the industry and make finding another job difficult. When the report came in it turned out that I had calculated and supplied more than five million board-feet of lumber to within inches of their requirements, and I had done it within budget. I was a hero. Morrison-Knudsen asked me to stay on. I was thrilled, but at the same time I knew that I owed much of my success to Jean's timely intervention. One job led to the next and by 1979 I rose to become Morrison-Knudsen's director of marketing in Hawaii.

Meanwhile problems were developing at home. Jean was working very hard and began talking about a vacation. I thought it was a terrific idea, at first. I assumed that she was considering a trip to one of the islands or perhaps to the mainland to visit Lynn and Doug. One day she brought home a bunch of travel brochures for Fiji! For some reason I had never thought that she wanted to travel out of the country. To go to Fiji required a passport, and a passport, in turn, required proof of citizenship. I had to have a birth certificate to get a passport. Since I had no such documents, of course, the vacation to Fiji was out of the question. But what could I tell Jean? First, I said that it was too much money. She waved that argument aside and showed me how inexpensive the trip really was. Then I complained about not having enough time. Out came the calendar as she pointed out the large spaces in our schedules during the coming months. Next I pleaded fatigue, which she saw as an additional reason for the vacation. This went on for weeks. I would come up with a reason for not going to Fiji, and Jean would show me how ridiculous I was being. "Why are you fighting so hard?" she kept asking. "I'm not fighting," I would reply, "I just don't feel like going to Fiji." "But why not?" "Just because!" And so it went. Jean knew that there had to be a reason for such nonsense, but for the life of her, she couldn't imagine what it was. How could she have known that it simply revolved around my inability to get a passport? Jean finally threw up her hands and went alone. She had a wonderful trip to Fiji and aside from several evenings of looking at her photographs, the subject seldom came up again. But I knew that the seed had been planted; Jean was growing more and more troubled about me, and the Fiji fiasco only served to confirm her doubts. Something was very wrong in our lives.

Just when things settled down another problem appeared. Morrison-Knudsen offered me a wonderful opportunity. They had just secured a lucrative contract in Saudi Arabia and asked if I would go as a member of the supervisory team. The salary was impressive for those days, $3000 a month, but I knew I couldn't accept. I would have needed a passport. I made the mistake of mentioning the offer to Jean, who thought it was a terrific opportunity. I told her that I had decided against it. "Why?" she demanded. "Too far from home." She couldn't understand it. "But what a wonderful chance to see the world," she argued. "And besides, we could use the money." I was firm. I simply didn't want to go. "But why not?! You always loved to travel." We started another round of arguments. I told her that it was too hot in Saudi Arabia. She shook her head. Then I said that I didn't get along with some of the other members of the supervisory team. Jean wasn't convinced. Finally I said that I would be lonely away from her and she sneered. "I don't know what's wrong with you, Dennis, but I don't like it. First you wouldn't go to Fiji, and now it's Saudi Arabia. Something just isn't right here." She was correct, of course, and I wished that I had the courage to tell why.

Life on the surface went on as usual. I turned sixty in 1980 and experienced the normal trauma of examining my life: weighing successes against failures, pleasures against pain, and expectations against fulfillment. Whatever doubts I had about approaching senility and mortality were eased by the fact that I entered and won the King's Court Tennis Championship against excellent players half my age. I was doing very well at Morrison-Knudsen and had recently brought in a $5 million contract for a major construction project in Kauai. Jean's life had changed more than mine. She had just turned fifty-five and had the option as a state employee to take early retirement. After analyzing the pros and cons of her job she decided that eight years of supervising a backbreaking case load were sufficient. She accepted her pension and an outstanding achievement award from the State of Hawaii and began looking for a new career. A week later, in November, 1981, Jean became the executive director of the Hawaii Refugee Resettlement Organization, a large, nonprofit, federally funded program concerned with the thousands of Southeast Asians who were arriving in Hawaii. The new job required a lot of traveling for conferences, fund raising, and the like. Frequently for the next two years Jean flew to Chicago or New York and loved it. Part of her enthusiasm was due to the challenge of her job, but part of it was knowing that she was getting away from the tension of our deteriorating homelife.

We just weren't talking anymore. Both of us were absorbed by our careers and concerned about advancing old age, but the root of the problem was my unexplainable behavior. My past was becoming a festering sore and I was too locked in to change things. When she had a vacation coming, she instinctively chose to spend it with one of the kids: white-water rafting down the Colorado River with Mark, or a social visit with Lynn, Steve, and young Michael. We barely had a relationship to speak of, although to all our friends we looked like a busy, happy couple. I didn't recognize it at the time but Jean was showing real signs of emotional stress. The new job and the constant travel were taking a toll, as was our lack of communication. Suddenly there was a new crisis: Lynn had cancer. What began as a small mole on her collarbone was soon diagnosed as a rapidly spreading malignancy. Jean dropped everything, of course, and rushed to her daughter's side at Houston's renowned M. D. Anderson Hospital. Within days Lynn underwent surgery, and there was some doubt if she would survive. Thank God, the operation was successful and the spreading cancer was caught in time. Jean was badly shattered by the experience, however, and the trauma of almost losing her daughter stayed with her for years.

We were riding an emotional roller coaster. Our moods fluctuated sharply, seldom in the same direction. One day Jean would be depressed and I would be euphoric; the next day would see the reverse. We took trips around the islands to relax and bring our moods into "sync," but we seldom found ourselves on the same wavelength. We still played tennis occasionally and socialized but it was becoming an effort. Jean buried herself in the resettlement programs of Indochinese refugees, and I continued to chase large construction contracts for Morrison-Knudsen. When business was slow, I took on jobs for other companies, largely, I now realize, to keep me occupied and away from home. I put in a short stint as the marketing director for General Construction Company, trying to collect some $3 million in accounts receivable, and then as an estimator for Commercial Shelving to install computer flooring in a British observatory at the peak of Mt. Mauna Kea. Jean flew more and more often to New York to meet with agency colleagues to promote alien-related laws and programs. I wish that I had been able to tell her that the alien who most needed her help was me! We were both miserable but didn't know how to get out of it. We were approaching the edge of the final slide.

THERE WAS A change taking place in Hawaii as well. For generations the islands had been a haven for immigrants: Japanese, Chinese, Polynesian, Portuguese, Spanish, and Filipinos. More recently, as Jean knew from personal experience, they were arriving in droves from Laos, Vietnam,

Hong Kong, and Taiwan. Most, however, were legal aliens. The Reagan Administration lumped our problem with the epidemic of illegal Mexican immigrants crossing into California, Texas, and New Mexico, and decided to crack down in Hawaii as well. Washington dispatched a new headhunter to replace the former district director of the Immigration and Naturalization Service in Hawaii, named Sam Feldman, and all hell broke loose. He absurdly declared that there were 30,000-40,000 illegal aliens on the islands and set out to find them. A small army of INS agents was ordered into the field to root them out. What followed was a wholesale violation of civil rights across Hawaii. The papers were filled with stories of Feldman's crusade and the questionable procedures involved. Most people, including Jean, were outraged at his hard-line approach but I was genuinely frightened. It was only a matter of time until I was swept up in the process. I lived in fear for the next two years until early 1984, when the growing number of lawsuits against the INS caused a Federal court to bring Feldman's campaign to a halt. It was hardly an atmosphere conducive to revealing my fugitive status.

In 1982 Jean started talking about planning for our social security benefits. I was nearly sixty-two and it seemed like a good thing to do. Besides, I thought it might provide us with a chance to mend fences. Little did I realize where it would lead. She began by sending off for her birth certificate and discovered that it had been lost in a courthouse fire in Red Bluff, California. I didn't realize when she embarked on the project that our birth certificates were required or I wouldn't have been as enthusiastic. Fortunately, it turned out to be a lengthy process, which gave me a lot of time to think of excuses when my turn came to produce my birth certificate. Jean spent months corresponding with the California Bureau of Vital Statistics trying to obtain a duplicate. First they wanted confirmation of her identity, then they sent the letters back to be notarized. More weeks passed, and they asked for her parents' names and birth dates. It was a circus. I watched with growing apprehension at the amount of red tape it took to get a simple birth certificate. My God, what would happen if I got into a similar mess? I hoped that Jean would get frustrated enough with the bureaucracy to call a halt to the project before it became my turn. Finally, nearly a year later, Jean's duplicate certificate arrived in the mail. She had done her part, and it was now my turn.

I stalled. I pretended to forget to write away for my papers. Hardly an evening passed that she didn't ask if I had mailed off a request. I tried to change the subject or pretend that I hadn't heard. At the beginning she just figured that I had other problems on my mind, but soon it became a corrosive issue. "Why are you being so lazy?" she asked. "Don't you care about your retirement benefits? Sure, it's a hassle, but it's the only way we can get our social security package together." Maybe I just didn't understand what was required, and she would painstakingly go over the process again. Sometimes I planned it so that I came home too late to discuss the matter. It was the passport situation all over again. After a while I simply told her that I had written off to the state capital of New York (which I learned was Albany) and that we would hear from them eventually. She was pleased that I had finally done something. I knew that the crisis was far from over but I was willing to risk it for a month or two of relief.

After six weeks of silence from Albany, Jean decided to take matters into her own hands. Now I was getting seriously worried. Jean was persistent and, as the Marine commandant had learned, not particularly frightened by authority figures. Now where was the capital of New York? Oh yes, Albany. Off went the letter, and I waited in dread for the obvious answer. It came several weeks later. They never heard of me. Jean fired off another letter that minced no words about the low level of competence among state bureaucrats. The answer was the same, only less polite. Jean couldn't understand it. I tried to shrug it off and wondered aloud if my years as an orphan at the Connecticut School for Boys hadn't caused me to be listed in that state instead. Jean wasted no time in writing Hartford. The reply was the same. She was totally bewildered and began to ask questions. "Tell me more about where you were born." "What were your folks' names again?" "How old were you when they were killed in the car crash?" I was getting panicky. Every answer entrapped me further. "What was the name of that Catholic school?" "The Connecticut School for Boys." "Where is it located?" "Jean! Who remembers? I was just a kid!" It went on for weeks. Finally Jean wrote to Hartford for the correct address. This time she learned that there was no such school. What the hell was going on here? All I could do was clam up. More weeks passed and the lies were hanging thick in the air. We continued to act normally around our friends and pursue our jobs, but our relationship was in tatters.

Our situation was complicated by the fact that business conditions had caused me to be laid off, and money was getting tight. Several months went by and I just couldn't seem to find work. Jean was growing resentful about being the perpetual breadwinner and finally convinced me to approach our upstairs neighbor, who was a successful real estate developer. After all, she reminded me, I had a good reputation in the trade; it wasn't like taking charity. To her relief he offered me a supervisory job on one of his construction sites. Maybe now our lives would get back to normal. When I reported for work I learned that the job was inside a military base and that I would soon be expected to submit to a security clearance check. Of course I couldn't do that, and after four days—"Four days!" Jean shrieked—I came home to tell her I had quit. I gave her a lame story about getting nauseous around the aviation fuel. Jean snapped. That was it! She was at the end of the line.

Jean suggested that we seek help. She knew the name of a highly respected psychiatrist in downtown Honolulu, Dr. Mark Bernstein, who could give us some marriage counseling. I reluctantly agreed to do it on a trial basis. That walk down the hall to his office was more frightening than the retreat toward Tunis in North Africa. Every cell in my body was alert for a slip-up. I couldn't imagine a greater threat than sitting in a darkened, fashionable office, alone, with Dr. Bernstein: a soft-spoken and skillful therapist whose goal was to ferret out the very secrets that I had spent my life covering up. I was in agony. I blocked and parried his questions. He asked me back for another visit. This time Dr. Bernstein hammered away at my relationship with Jean. I assured him that I loved her and that she was certainly not at fault. During the next visit his manner changed abruptly. "Did you kill your parents?" he suggested suddenly. "No, no, nothing like that," I said, although in a manner of speaking I had declared them dead when I escaped from Deming so many years before. I made that my last visit. Jean, however, continued her sessions although it was clear that I was the problem. Our relationship, complicated by her stressful job, Lynn's recent cancer, and the growing resentment of carrying the financial burden, was driving her toward a nervous breakdown. Since I had announced that I wanted no part in further therapy, it was clear that things would only become worse.

One evening in March 1982, Jean and I sat down to discuss our bleak future. It was apparent that I was also at the end of my rope. I had been frightened my entire adult life. I had fought intimacy. I had spent my waking moments rehearsing cover stories. This time there was no talking my way out of it. I was about to lose everything: wife-protector-companion-safe harbor. The most tragic part was that I really loved Jean. I really did. Oh, I could make it by myself, if I had to. I could stay in the construction business or even become a professional artist. In fact, I could probably do well at any job that didn't require detailed forms or a security clearance. I might even go back to the tennis business, although I had to be careful not to get my picture into the paper. I was also forced to admit that Jean would probably fare better without me. She was resilient: a hard-working professional and a fun-loving companion. I knew she would come out of this crisis intact, probably better than I would. This was clearly the deathknell of our marriage. Jean begged for some concession but all I could do was sit on the couch in silence. Our last opportunity for some sort of reconciliation had passed.

When the futility of our discussion became clear we sadly agreed that the only solution was divorce. Jean reluctantly went to the bedroom to begin packing her suitcases. She was leaving. All I could seem to do was stand on the balcony of our condominium and stare at the sunset beyond Lahi Lahi Point. It was all over.

I was jarred out of my reverie by the sound of the doorbell and turned back to the living room to see Jean, her bags packed, waiting for the taxi. I watched, almost dumbstruck, as she handed her luggage to the driver. God, if I had only handled this differently! Why hadn't I told her the truth in the beginning? I started crying. The taxi driver was wrestling her bags toward the elevator. As she was about to leave she turned in the doorway—I could see the tears from across the room—and made one last try. "Are you some kind of criminal, Dennis?"

This was my final chance and I knew it. Shaking with emotion, I broke and admitted that I was a fugitive. I was a German soldier. I was wanted by the FBI for the last thirty-seven years. I remember covering my face to control my hysterical sobbing as the dike finally burst and the whole story came tumbling out. We spent the rest of the long night sitting in the kitchen, alternately crying and laughing, as I told the first person in my life who I really was.

The next day we went together to the public library in Waianae where I showed her on the map where I was born. I traced the fighting across North Africa and pointed out my prison camps in America. She just kept shaking her head in wonderment and squeezing my arm. She kept repeating "It's O.K." "It's O.K."

Over the next few days Jean and I chattered non-stop as I tried to tell her about my life. All my quirks suddenly made sense to her. She was relieved to see that she wasn't at fault in the deterioration of our marriage. Then we faced the question of my legal position and the alternatives I might pursue. We agreed that I wasn't a hardened criminal, after all, and that my case was probably unique. I was brought to the United States against my will as a military prisoner. Moreover, I had escaped at the urging of my government no differently than American POWs did in Germany. Movies were made about the heroes who tunneled out of Stalag XVII. Since I escaped from Deming after the war was over, there might even be some question if I was still a prisoner of war. I didn't break any laws during my escape or since, and paid my taxes every year, even if under a different name. Surely, they wouldn't deport me to Germany or Poland after all these years?! We came to two conclusions: I would surrender to the authorities after my story— this book—was published; and Jean would support me whatever the outcome. How lucky I am to have her.

A few days later Jean suggested that I write to the German Red Cross to see if *we* had any living relatives, and a month later learned to my astonishment that my sister, Lotte, now in her mid-sixties, was alive in Braunschweig, West Germany! Overjoyed, we made contact and sobbed together with a woman nearly five thousand miles away who had thought I was dead for four decades. I learned that my family had suffered terribly under the Russians. They were separated and forced to do farm labor for Poles who had been imported to Schweidnitz, renamed Swidnica, by the Russians. Eventually, Papa was able to smuggle the family to West Germany. My brother, Paul, died in the early 1950s, and my parents lived into the early 1960s in Braunschweig. "Mother and Father never gave up hope that you had survived," Lotte shouted in broken English. "Papa even placed advertisements in the major German and American newspapers. To the end of their lives they kept your picture on the dining room table. They never gave up hope that you were alive and happy and free."

INDEX

180

Mt. Disney, runs on, 87–88
Tim, 88

Tamura, Cliff, 166
Tamura, Mr., 166
Taylor, Elizabeth, 93
Techner, Bill, 81
Tennis magazine, 149
Tennis moves, analysis of, 149
"Tennis Scene," 154
Tennyson, Lord Alfred, 41
Tilden, Bill, 40, 81, 93
Tim, the bartender, 88, 91
Total Tennis, 149
Tournaments, tennis, 82, 155, 156, 158,
    159, 160, 166, 172
Towne Realty Company, 168–69
Traybert, Tony, 159
Trispel, Horst, 38, 41–43, 136
Trumbul, Mary D., 120
Tunisia, 48
Tyre, Morris, 103

University of California:
  at Berkeley, 114
  Lodge, 90
  at Santa Barbara, 151
U.S. Lawn Tennis Association, 156, 158

Van Dillon, Eric, 160
Vokietatis, Al, 125
Völkischer Beobachter, Die, 49
Von Cramm, Gottfried, 114
Von Muller, Ursula, 38, 41

Waianae, Hawaii, 177
Washington, Ill., 121
Wehrmacht Officers' School, 127
Weiner Neustadt, 48
Welch, Lowell, 115, 126, 131, 154
Welch, Yvonne, 154
Westphal, Kurt Richard, 122, 124, 150
Whiles, Dennis, origin of name, 72–77
Wiisanen, Wayne, 125
Wilson, Dorothy, 117, 142
Wilson, Lionel, 117, 126, 142
"Windjammer, The," 147
Wolff, Carla, 99–100, 112
Wonder Department Store, 82
World War II, outbreak, 41

Yosemite, 89
Youth "culture," 143–45

Zephyr Cove, Nev., 136
Zimbalist, Efram, Jr., 155